soft+simple knits for little ones

HEIDI BOYD

Photography by Brian Steege

NORTH LIGHT BOOKS

CINCINNATI, OHIO

11 10 09 08 07   5 4 3 2 1

Distributed in Canada by Fraser Direct
100 Armstrong Avenue
Georgetown, ON, Canada L7G 5S4
Tel: (905) 877-4411

Distributed in the U.K. and Europe by David & Charles
Brunel House, Newton Abbot, Devon, TQ12 4PU, England
Tel: (+44) 1626 323200, Fax: (+44) 1626 323319
Email: postmaster@davidandcharles.co.uk

Distributed in Australia by Capricorn Link
P.O. Box 704, S. Windsor, NSW 2756 Australia
Tel: (02) 4577-3555

Library of Congress Cataloging-in-Publication Data

Boyd, Heidi
   Soft + simple knits for little ones : over 45 easy patterns / by Heidi Boyd ; photography by Brian Steege. -- 1st ed.
      p. cm.
   Includes index.
   ISBN-13: 978-1-58180-965-7
   1. Knitting--Patterns. 2. Infants' clothing. 3. Children's clothing. I. Title.
   TT825.B658 2007
   746.43'2041--dc22
                        2007021362

Editor: Jessica Gordon
Designer: Maya Drozdz
Production Coordinator: Greg Nock
Technical Editor: Alexandra Virgiel
Technical Illustrator: Toni Toomey
Photographers: Brian Steege + Christine Polomsky
Stylist: Monica Skrzelowski
Make-up Artist: Cass Smith

Metric Conversion Chart

to convert	to	multiply by
Inches	Centimeters	2.54
Centimeters	Inches	0.4
Feet	Centimeters	30.5
Centimeters	Feet	0.03
Yards	Meters	0.9
Meters	Yards	1.1
Sq. Inches	Sq. Centimeters	6.45
Sq. Centimeters	Sq. Inches	0.16
Sq. Feet	Sq. Meters	0.09
Sq. Meters	Sq. Feet	10.8
Sq. Yards	Sq. Meters	0.8
Sq. Meters	Sq. Yards	1.2
Pounds	Kilograms	0.45
Kilograms	Pounds	2.2
Ounces	Grams	28.3
Grams	Ounces	0.035

fw
F+W PUBLICATIONS, INC.

www.fwbookstore.com

DEDICATION

To my three little ones, Jasper, Elliot and Celia…who are all not so little anymore…you'll always be my precious babies even when I have to look up to see your faces!

And to my darling husband, this wild ride wouldn't be the same without you in the driver's seat beside me.

ACKNOWLEDGMENTS

In moments of serious doubt and confusion, providence and good fortune landed me in our fabulous local knitting shop, The Knitting Experience Café, where I found not only a wealth of information but friendship and an unending source of encouragement as well. The owner, Chesley Flotten, got me started by placing interchangeable needles and irresistibly soft yarn in my hands. Attending the store's Knit-at-Night helped set my course and made me understand what designs knitters were looking for. Near the end of the book, when it seemed like I would never finish, Chesley came to the rescue by graciously contributing beautiful projects, which I can't wait to knit up myself. I'm ever so grateful for her support and guidance. Celia is a big fan, too—she loves eating the store's cookies and rearranging the knitting baskets, making the shop one of our very favorite places to frequent.

I'd also like to thank the following knitters, without whose help I never would have made my deadline: Becka Homan, who contributed the adorable toddler mittens; Jean Herlihy, who would exchange work with me at our sons' basketball games; and Melissa Orth, the fabulous knitting librarian. Most especially I'd like to thank my editor, Jessica Gordon, who answers countless questions and transforms my copy into legible text.

contents

confessions of a knitter-mama

Until I started working on this book, I'd put aside my needles for almost fifteen years because I didn't think I had time to knit. The challenge of writing this book brought me back into the wonderful world of knitting. All of a sudden I was in the enviable position of being able to carve knitting time into my day and justify it as work, truly an amazing opportunity—sorry, honey, I can't do the dishes, vacuum or put in a load of laundry. I have to get back to "work"!

Then the panic set in. How was I going to get this all done in one year with a six-month-old daughter (who's now a busy toddler) and her two much older brothers, all needing lots of attention? I found myself in some pretty humorous situations. My husband laughed to see me with my needles carefully poised above baby Celia, sleeping in my lap. And I had to giggle at myself stealing a few frantic minutes of knitting when Celia conked out in the car seat as we waited for Elliot or Jasper to come out of lessons or practice.

Although motherhood was the greatest hurdle in getting the work done for this book, my experiences with our children were the best assets in designing projects. I have years of firsthand experience clothing children. I've lived through trying to get them dressed up for special occasions when they want to stay in shorts and a T-shirt (thankfully, casual life in Maine makes this an infrequent ordeal). I've stayed up washing favorite outfits while they sleep so they can wear them again the next morning (when there's a dresser full of perfectly fine clothes ready and waiting). I've also tried without much success to make them put on extra layers before they go out in the cold.

The wonderful thing about comfortable, fun clothes and accessories is that not only do they make the kids look great, they make a parent's job easy. Putting a bear hat (see page 36) on a toddler while teaching him how to growl works like a gem. Pulling on a fleecy-soft shark sweater (see page 94) that's chasing a small fish on the back starts a fun game of running in circles that distracts them from complaining. Girls who might refuse to wear a scarf will think it's fun to wear a *Foxy Stole* (see page 120), and they'll get a kick out of wearing shaggy leg warmers, too (see page 128). Wearing a matching felted crown with your slippers (see page 108) elevates simply keeping your feet warm around the house into a fun dress-up game.

As much as I adored dressing my two boys, it's awfully fun to have the chance to dress a little girl. At one and a half, Celia is already passionate about shoes, jewelry, "hair pretties" and fancy trims on her clothes. She was the inspiration for many of the clothes and accessories in this book. We can't wait to get the originals back and put them to use. She was especially interested in the butterfly purse and squirrel tote (see page 146). They are the perfect size for stowing away little books and treasures. When I finished the faces of the *Fairy-Tale Dolls* (see page 54), she crushed them with great big hugs—it will be a happy reunion when they come home. Before I know it she'll be ready to dress them herself.

Once I got to the end of the book I was having so much fun I didn't want to stop…actually extra pages had to be added because I couldn't stop. It was just so gratifying to see how many beautiful projects could be whipped together in very little time. The most important discovery was that knitting really is family-friendly. Unlike other crafting pursuits, you can be in the hub of activity and still make progress.

So here's my challenge to you: If I can find a way to keep the kids fed, clothed and happy (in varying degrees) and knit almost all of these projects in less than a year, you should at the very least be able to relax and take pleasure in knitting one or two. My hope is you enjoy knitting them so much that you'll make a few more.

Best of luck and happy hours of knitting.

❀ CHOOSING yarn

To someone who loves color and texture, yarn shops are a field day of inspiration. Wall-to-wall luscious fibers in vibrant colors can make narrowing your selection difficult. It's hard to know where to start. The easiest route is to select the pattern first and stick with the specified yarn. Matching the exact yarn manufacturer and blend will help guarantee successful results. However, you can also substitute yarns. The following information will educate you about the different types and weights of yarn.

yarn weight key

a. super bulky
B. chunky/bulky
C. worsted
D. sport
e. heavy worsted
F. worsted
G. novelty
H. bulky novelty

yarn weights

If you want to substitute yarn, the first step is to select a yarn similar in weight to what's listed in the pattern. There is a standard yarn weight system compiled by the Craft Yarn Council of America (see the chart on page 153), but not every manufacturer uses the standardized system. The picture and yarn key below show you what the different weights of yarn look like.

The majority of the projects in this book feature yarns in the middle of the weight chart. The delicate baby yarns that used to be so popular for baby gifts require tiny needles and are just too time-consuming for most knitters. Worsted weight is my personal favorite choice for knitting sweaters for babies, toddlers and older children. This middle-weight yarn lets them move freely while still providing adequate warmth. Knitting on the companion size six to size nine needles keeps the project going at a good pace.

yarn fibers

The next concern is to be aware of the fiber content of the original yarn and try to find a similar blend. All fibers behave differently. Some have natural elasticity while others may have very limited flexibility.

In general, synthetic fibers such as acrylic and nylon are less expensive and are easily washable. Man-made fibers can be incredibly soft and tempting, but they often lack the richness and durability of natural fibers. Common natural fibers include wool, alpaca, cotton, bamboo and even soy. In many cases, natural fibers are more expensive and more complicated to launder. For children's clothing, look for creative fiber blends that offer the advantages of both varieties, fibers that are machine washable, durable and—above all else—comfortable.

yarn yardage

Yardage is another factor to keep in mind while yarn shopping. All skeins of yarn are not created equal. For instance, it takes only two skeins of Malabrigo to make the *Swing Jacket* (see page 74), and two skeins of Lorna's Laces to make the *Tie-On Asymmetrical Sweater* (see page 70). Both of these yarns have packed an incredible length into their skeins. Usually it would take at least four regular-sized skeins to make a similarly sized child's sweater. At first glance, Malabrigo and Lorna's Laces may seem expensive, but when you begin comparing the yarns based on yardage, you'll find that the price is fair, especially for the high quality of the yarn.

The heavy weight of a bulky skein can be deceptive. It takes three skeins of Blue Sky Alpacas Bulky Hand Dyes yarns to make the preschool backpack (see page 142) and two whole skeins of Berroco Hip-Hop to make the small slippers and crown set (see page 108). It should be noted that both projects are felted, a shrinking process that gobbles up yardage.

At any rate, make sure to compare the yardage of the original specified yarn to the one you're substituting. Most of the projects in the book require around four skeins of yarn, but many require only two or three skeins.

Experienced knitters know the importance of buying slightly more yarn than they need for a project. The reason for this is that no two dye lots are ever exactly the same. If you're knitting a project that has many different colors, a change in dye lot may be barely noticeable. But if you're knitting a solid-colored blanket or sweater and you run out of yarn, the addition of a new skein from a different dye lot may create an odd change in hue and may detract from the look of your beautiful knitting. If you end up with too much yarn, most stores will accept returns within a specified amount of time, so there's really no reason not to err on the safe side.

Whenever you're able, take advantage of the expertise in your local yarn store. Most people who work in and own shops are experienced knitters and are very familiar with the yarns they carry. I ask questions wherever I go, and I couldn't have finished the book if it weren't for the yarn suggestions of many store owners and yarn manufacturers.

gauge

Once you've selected the yarn, it's time to check your gauge. I have to confess that when I was knitting sweaters in college I didn't take the time to knit up gauge swatches. To this day some of those gigantic sweaters still exist packed away in a storage box (I did use one when I was nine months pregnant with our first son). Spare yourself the grief of making a garment that won't fit. I'm now keenly aware of how an entire pattern hinges on your gauge, which is simply the length and width measurement of stitches and rows.

Using the specified needles and yarn, knit up a small 4" (10cm) test swatch. When you're finished, carefully measure it and compare your measurement with the stipulated gauge. If necessary, adjust the needle size, either up to enlarge your stitch or down to narrow it. This simple step is all you need to do to ensure that you knit a garment that fits. When it comes to substituting yarn, the gauge piece will also give you a sense of how the yarn will work with the pattern.

ᎶᎪᏖᎻᎬᏒᎥᏁᎶ TOOLS

I'm surrounded by so much stuff—toys, clothes, sports equipment and musical instruments—that I really strive for simplicity in my own pursuits. That's why the following is a very minimal list of what you need to get started with knitting. This is a hobby intended for your enjoyment, so really purchase what makes you happy. There are gorgeous tote bags, silk project bags and even woven baskets for your projects. Sometimes I'm tempted by the bamboo knitting needles packaged in beautiful silk cases or artful tin canisters. Of course, if you do stick with just the basics, then you don't have to feel guilty if you go hog wild purchasing all those irresistible yarns.

needles

INTERCHANGEABLE KNITTING NEEDLES SET

I hate to find myself ready to launch into a project with the perfect yarn and pattern in hand only to find I don't have the right size needles and the stores are closed. This is only one of the reasons why I love having a Denise Interchangeable Knitting Needles Kit at the ready. Compared to buying individual needles, it's a great value. When the pattern calls for a change in needle size, you simply twist off the needle ends and replace them with a size smaller or larger. If your project starts out bigger, like the rib edge for a hat, and then narrows on the way to the top, you can use one of the connectors to effortlessly slide your stitches onto a smaller cord so you can continue knitting in the round. The kit also provides end caps that transform the cords into straight needles or stitch holders.

WOODEN NEEDLES AND BAMBOO NEEDLES

Lots of people have told me wooden or bamboo needles are the best for beginners. I can see how they would be less slippery and warmer than the old-fashioned metal needles I started out with when I was five. The hardness and smoothness of bamboo needles are indeed luxurious. Companies like Lantern Moon create needles made of inlaid wood that are like functional pieces of art.

DOUBLE-POINTED NEEDLES

Double-pointed needles, or DPNs, have points on either end and are intended for knitting in the round. Divide the stitches evenly onto four needles and use the fifth needle to start working your way around, knitting each set of stitches onto a new needle.

CIRCULAR NEEDLES

Circular needles are simply two straight needle points joined by a flexible cord. They make knitting a round tube effortless. They're so versatile, I use them instead of straight needles even when knitting flat pieces. I love the way the needles curl up and travel so easily. I'm so addicted to knitting with circulars, I don't even own a set of double-pointed needles. I simply use two sets of circular needles to knit sleeves, leg warmers, hats and even mittens. See page 16 for step-by-step illustrations of this simple and effective technique. I'm sure this is probably considered unorthodox knitting, and savvy knitters all over are rolling their eyes at my naiveté. The only drawback I've found is that it's a little harder to pull the connections tight between the circulars as opposed to using traditional double-pointed needles. In my child-centered world, circulars are safer—little fingers can't resist pulling out all four of the tempting DPNs.

from bottom left: two sets of five double-pointed needles, circular needles with different-sized cables in and out of pockets, retractable cloth tape measure, straight needles in pockets. Knitting needle case, darker wood needles and tape measure by Lantern Moon.

ADDITIONAL TOOLS

STITCH HOLDERS

Stitch holders are like big safety pins that hold live stitches until you're ready to work with them. You need a few different-sized holders in your stash: Use small holders for shoulder and strap stitches, and use larger holders for neck stitches. In a pinch you can always transfer stitches onto a scrap of yarn with a tapestry needle. It's just quicker and more convenient to pass the holder's metal tip through the stitches.

STITCH MARKERS

Stitch markers make your life so easy. I often forget to use them and find myself tediously counting stitches trying to figure out when I should begin the color chart or knit stitches together. They can be simple plastic washers or ornate metal loops with pretty glass beads. All you really need is a large enough opening to slide onto your needle. Or just knot a contrasting color of yarn and slide it over the needle—it may not be fancy, but it'll do the trick.

GAUGE RULE AND NEEDLE SIZER

This combination ruler and needle sizer is a staple in any knitter's arsenal of tools. Some gauge rulers even have a central cutout that allows you to quickly measure your gauge over 4" (10cm). The rows of needle-sized holes help you establish the size of any unmarked needle.

MEASURING TAPE

A cloth measuring tape is a must. Almost all the patterns require you to knit for a specified number of inches. Only a cloth tape will lie directly against your knitting to get an accurate measurement.

YARN (DARNING) NEEDLES

Make sure you have a selection of these blunt-tipped needles with large eyes for weaving in loose ends and seaming together pieces. I like the varieties that come with a little tube-shaped carrying case for safekeeping.

SCISSORS

I don't know how or why my scissors disappear whenever I'm ready to snip the yarn. Some yarns simply refuse to tear and you really do need a nice, clean cut if you're threading the end through a tapestry needle. Keep a folding pair of scissors in your project bag, and don't let anyone know they're in there.

ZIPPERED PROJECT BAGS

These plastic bags that zipper shut are just like the clear bags linens are sold in. They're stronger and bigger than zippered kitchen bags and still have the advantage of letting you see what's in them. Keep both the yarn and your knitting in the bag to protect them from coffee spills, pet hair or any other potential incidents of daily life. At one point in the height of knitting for this book, I had a large wooden crate filled with loaded project bags so I could quickly grab the one I felt like knitting on my way out the door.

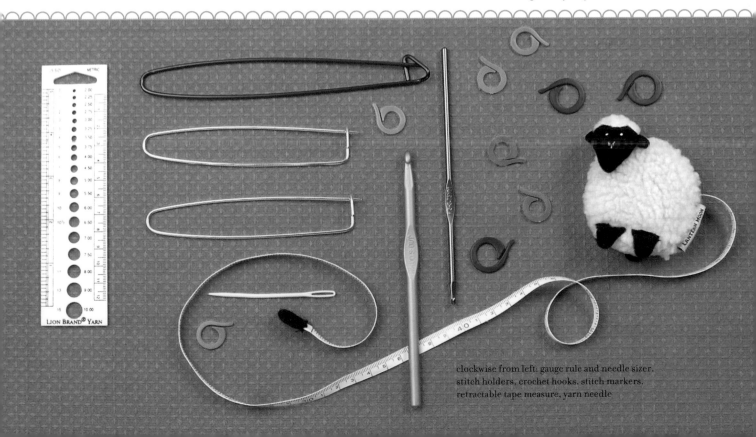

clockwise from left: gauge rule and needle sizer, stitch holders, crochet hooks, stitch markers, retractable tape measure, yarn needle

Learning the Basics

I'm always saddened to hear how frustrated some of my friends have become when learning how to knit. I think the solution is to find instruction that suits your learning style. If you can easily interpret diagrams and written instructions, the following pages should set you on your course. If not, there are many other avenues to look to for guidance and information. My first suggestion would be to visit your local yarn shop to get some experienced hands-on help. Many shops and local adult education programs offer beginning courses that teach knitting basics. Don't overlook your television or computer either—check your listings for knitting programming or search online for instructional downloads. It may take a combination of two or more of these sources to reach your eureka moment, but once you get there you'll see that it really is easy after all. Knitters are always learning from each other, so never be shy about asking questions; in my experience, knitters love to share their enthusiasm and knowledge of the craft.

CASTING ON LONG-TAIL STYLE

This is the most common way to cast on stitches. It might seem a little awkward to hold the yarn this way and hook the needle tip through each loop, but once you get the hang of it, you'll be amazed how quickly the stitches add up. This technique creates a nice clean cast-on edge at the bottom of your knitting.

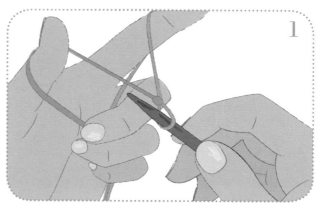

1. MAKE SLIP KNOT AND POSITION YARN
Make a slip knot, leaving a long tail (at least 2" [5cm] for every 1" [3cm] you'll be casting on) and slide it onto the needle with the long tail dangling from the front of the needle. Slide your thumb and index finger between the two strands of yarn, and wrap the tail around your thumb and the strand still attached to the skein around your index finger. Catch both strands under your remaining fingers to provide stability.

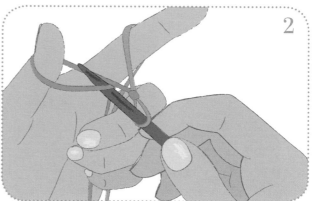

2. BRING NEEDLE UNDER AND OVER FRONT STRAND
Bring the needle tip under the strand of yarn in front of your thumb, then over the strand behind your thumb.

3. GRAB SECOND STRAND
Bring the needle behind the strand of yarn on the front of your index finger and "grab" it with the needle tip.

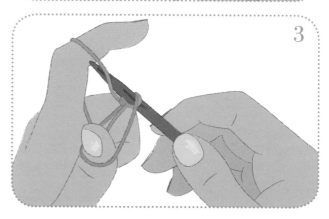

4. DRAW BACK STRAND THROUGH FRONT LOOP

Bring the yarn back through the loop you created with your thumb, creating a second loop on your needle (your first cast-on stitch). Let the loop fall away from your thumb, then tug gently on the strands with thumb and index finger to tighten the loop. Keep your cast-on stitches on the looser side rather than tightening them excessively.

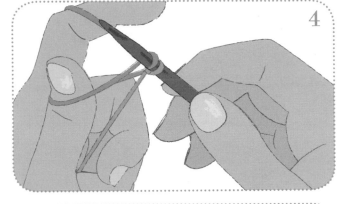

KNITTING CONTINENTAL

I wish I'd learned to knit this way from the start. This technique is not only faster but avoids the repetitive yarn-wrapping motion that over time may strain your wrists and fingers. When knitting continental you hold the yarn around your left forefinger and dip the right-hand needle tip into it before making a stitch. I find it especially quick to knit in the round using this technique—you just wrap the yarn around your fingertip once, and then keep on knitting. It takes a little more time to set it up when you're knitting a straight piece that needs to be flipped with each row.

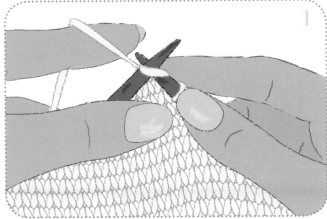

1. INSERT RIGHT NEEDLE INTO STITCH

With the yarn wrapped around or under your left index finger, insert the right needle into the first stitch on the left needle from front to back. The right-hand needle should cross behind the left-hand needle.

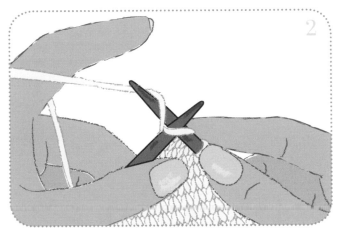

2. WRAP YARN WITH LEFT HAND

Place the right needle tip behind the yarn held in your left hand. The side of the needle facing you will be wrapped in yarn. Dip the needle tip down to begin pulling it through the stitch on the left needle.

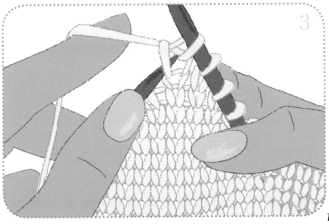

3. CREATE NEW STITCH

Pull the wrapped yarn through the stitch on the left needle, and bring the yarn up on the right needle to create a new stitch, allowing the old stitch to slide easily off sthe left-hand needle. The new stitch remains on the right-hand needle.

PURLING CONTINENTAL

Purling continental offers all the same advantages as knitting continental. In fact, the time savings seem even more no-ticeable. Purled rows are easily distinguished by the raised wavy pattern. When you knit, the bump is made at the back of the work where the yarn wraps around the needle. Conversely, when you purl the bump is in the front where yarn is held and wrapped. A purl row is intentionally added to many designs to add texture without using more complicated stitches.

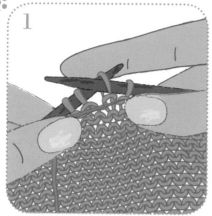
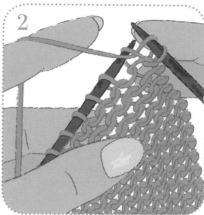

1. PREPARE TO PURL

Hold the working yarn in your left hand, and situate the stitches about ½" to 1" (1cm to 3cm) away from the tips of the needles. Slide the tip of the right-hand needle into the first stitch on the left-hand needle from back to front.

2. WRAP YARN AROUND NEEDLE

Use your left hand to wrap the work-ing yarn around the tip of the right-hand needle counterclockwise. Draw the right-hand needle back through the stitch, catching the wrapped work-ing yarn with the tip of the needle and bringing it back through the stitch on the left-hand needle.

3. CREATE PURL STITCH

Pull the old stitch off the left-hand needle, creating a new purl stitch on the right-hand needle. For illustration purposes, the working yarn is shown held between the index finger and thumb. However, when working an entire row without stopping, the yarn should remain in the position shown in step 2 to create proper tension.

INCREASING AND DECREASING

Increasing and decreasing allow you to shape your knitting to any size. Eliminating stitches makes the piece smaller, and adding stitches makes the piece larger. Once you've familiarized yourself with these basic shaping techniques, you're ready to shape any of the patterns in the book.

KNIT TWO TOGETHER (K2TOG)

This technique really is as simple as it sounds. By placing your needle tip through two stitches instead of one, you knit the stitches together into a single stitch. This technique is used repeatedly through many of the patterns to narrow the top of a hat, the end of a sleeve, or even to shape a stuffed animal's head.

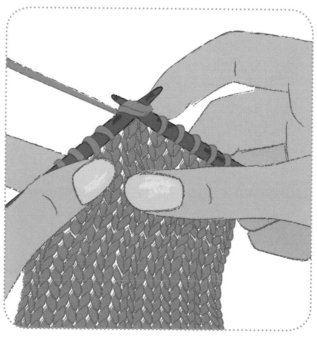

Slide the right-hand needle (from front to back, as for a regular knit stitch) into two stitches together, and knit them together as one stitch. You have decreased one stitch.

KNIT ONE FRONT AND BACK (KFB)

The title of this technique explains the process very clearly. By knitting a single stitch twice you create two stitches where there used to be one.

1. KNIT INTO FRONT OF STITCH

Slip the needle into the next stitch on the left-hand needle from front to back and knit the stitch as usual, but do not slip the stitch off the needle.

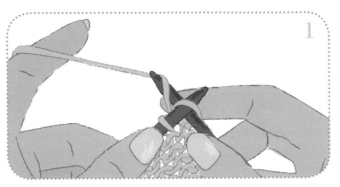

2. KNIT INTO BACK OF STITCH

Instead of slipping the stitch off the needle, bring the needle around to the back of the same stitch and knit another stitch.

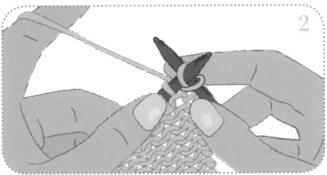

3. CREATE NEW STITCH

Slide both stitches off the needle, and you have created one new stitch.

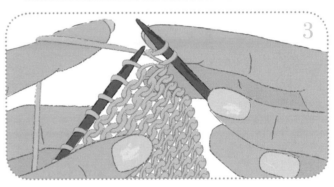

MAKE ONE

The make one increase is the most invisible way to add a stitch between two existing stitches. Most of the other increase techniques may create a hole where the stitch has been added. For this reason it's especially important to use a make one increase when working with smooth, solid-colored yarns.

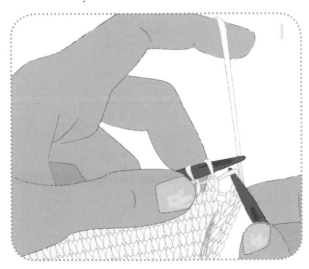

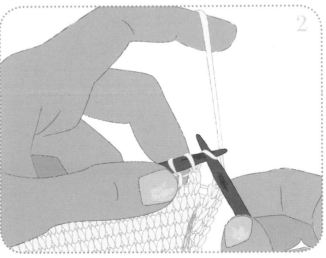

1. LIFT BAR

Slide the tip of the right-hand needle into the bar of the stitch directly before the next stitch to be knit on the left-hand needle. Slide this bar onto the left-hand needle.

2. KNIT NEW STITCH

Knit the new stitch through the back loop.

knitting in the round with two circular needles

I love this technique—it really simplifies and speeds up knitting in the round. Instead of separating your stitches between four double-pointed needles, you divide them in half between two circular needles. It's akin to knitting two separate straight pieces that share a skein of yarn. The key is that the stitches never transfer to the other circular needle. They slide down from one point of their circular needle to the other end to be reknitted back onto the same needle. The stitches are well protected between the needlepoints so you can easily set down your knitting and quickly pick it back up. The length of the needle cord allows you to expand your knitting so you can more accurately gauge size while in progress. If you're careful, you can even try on a hat or sock while it's still on the needles.

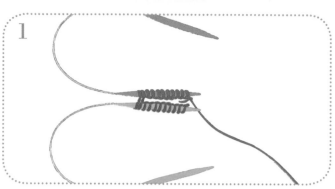

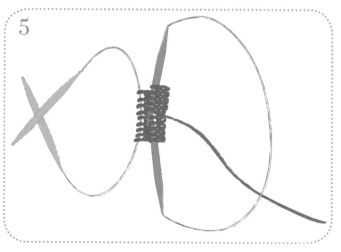

1. CAST ON STITCHES AND DIVIDE THEM

Cast on the full number of stitches onto one circular needle as instructed in the pattern. Slip half of the stitches as if to purl from one circular needle to a second circular needle. Move both sets of stitches to one end of each circular needle so the stitches line up.

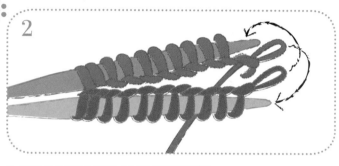

2. SWAP FIRST AND LAST STITCHES

Before joining the stitches, slip the first stitch from the back needle onto the front needle, and slip the first stitch from the front needle onto the back needle so the two stitches trade places. Switching the position of the stitches in this way will help stop the tube from gaping at the join.

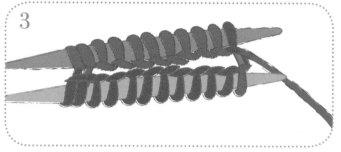

3. JOIN STITCHES

Grab the needle end attached to the front needle (shown in pink above). Slip the tip of the needle into the first stitch on the front needle (pink) to prepare for a knit stitch. Grab the working yarn attached to the back needle (shown in blue above) and knit.

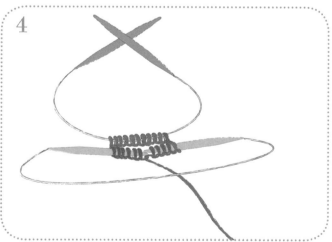

4. CONTINUE TO KNIT ON FRONT NEEDLE

Continue knitting all the stitches on the front needle, The back needle (shown in blue above) rests at the back of the work. After you have knitted all the stitches on the front needle, allow the stitches to rest on the cable of the front needle and rotate the work so that the back needle (shown in blue) comes to the front.

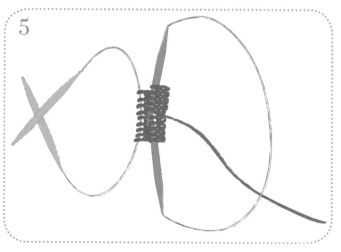

5. CONTINUE KNITTING IN A TUBE

Knit the stitches on the new front needle (shown in blue above). Keep rotating the work after you finish knitting the stitches on the needle in front, always using only the needle in front. You will produce a knitted Stockinette stitch tube, where the right side of the fabric is on the outside of the tube, and the wrong side of the fabric is on the inside.

KNITTING I-CORD

It still amazes me how easy it is to knit a three-dimensional piece without connecting the stitches and working in the round. By simply sliding the stitches down to the other end of the double-pointed (or circular) needles, you force them to create a nifty little tube. I-cords can be knitted in all different sizes and lengths and make handy ties, drawstrings, handles and even clever little topknots for stretchy hats.

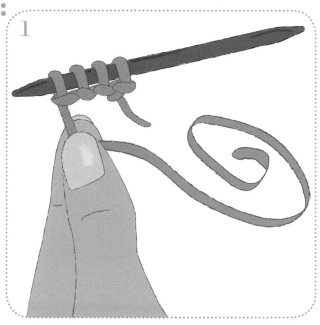

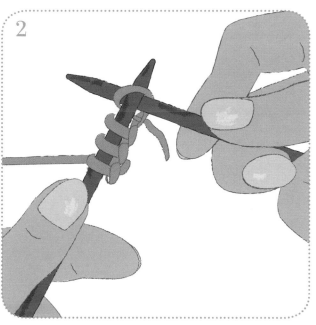

1. CAST ON STITCHES

Cast on the required number of stitches onto one DPN. Two to four stitches works best.

2. PREPARE FOR FIRST STITCH

Slide the stitches down the DPN so the first cast-on stitch is at one end of the DPN. The working yarn should be farthest from the point.

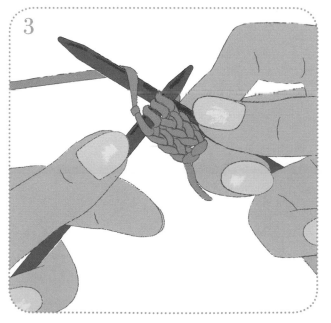

3. KNIT I-CORD

Pull the working yarn from the last stitch to the first stitch and knit. Continue knitting all stitches. Instead of turning the entire needle when you finish a row (as for regular knitting), simply slide all the stitches to the end of the needle again. Do not turn your work at all at any time. Keep pulling the working yarn behind the tube that forms to the first stitch in each row. Pretty soon you'll have a lovely tube—without having purled a stitch, and without ever turning your work.

Intarsia

I'm always surprised to hear how many people are hesitant to change colors and knit images into their work. It really is very easy—it's just a matter of knitting stitches in a different color of yarn. To begin, wind a short length of accent color(s) onto a bobbin (or loop a length around your fingertips, and then wind around the center of the loops). Following the color chart, switch to knitting from the bobbin/looped yarn for the required number of stitches. You'll find the intarsia patterns in this book are intended for beginners and only require one to two color changes. It's the perfect way to get started with this technique.

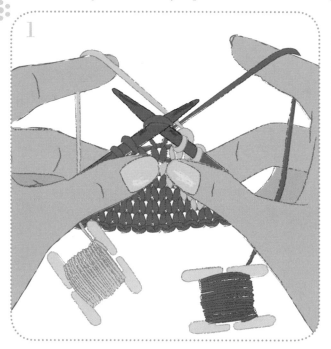

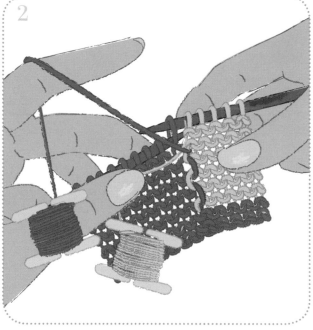

1. TWIST COLORS FROM RIGHT SIDE

When switching from one color to another with the right side facing, twist the old color and new color around each other behind the work to prevent gaps.

2. TWIST COLORS FROM WRONG SIDE

Twist the yarns around each other in the same manner when the back of the work is facing you.

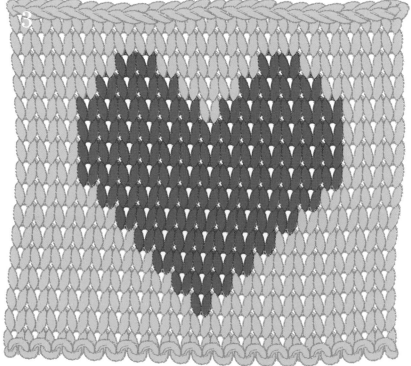

3. INTARSIA IN PROGRESS

From the front of the piece, your work will look like this as you progress. Notice the switches in color are seamless—there are no holes in the work. When weaving in the loose ends be sure to weave them behind a matching color block so they're virtually invisible on both the front and the back.

BINDING OFF

All good things must come to an end so they can be worn. Obviously you can't just slip live stitches off your needle—if you did, your work would completely unravel. The binding off process loops one stitch into another, stabilizing the edge of your work. It's very important to be aware of your tension while binding off. If you pull the stitches too tightly, you can pucker the top of your knitting and restrict its ability to stretch.

1. KNIT TWO STITCHES
Knit the first two stitches in the row just as you would for a normal knitted row.

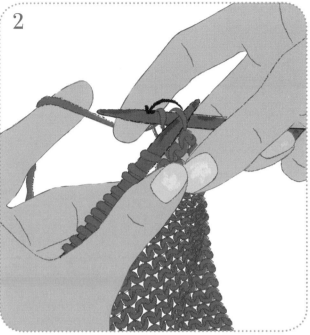

2. PASS FIRST STITCH OVER SECOND STITCH
Insert the left-hand needle into the first knitted stitch and pass that stitch over the second knitted stitch.

3. BIND OFF FIRST STITCH
There is now one less stitch on the right-hand needle.

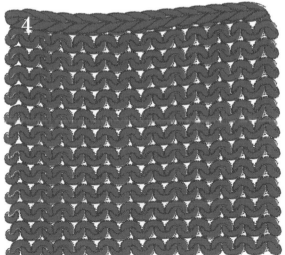

4. CONTINUE TO BIND OFF ALL STITCHES
To bind off the next stitch, knit one more stitch (two stitches on right-hand needle), then pass the preceding stitch over that one. Continue to knit one stitch and then pass the preceding stitch over it until you have bound off all the stitches. Cut the yarn and pull the tail through the final stitch.

mattress stitch

The good news is that many of the projects in this book are knit in the round or knit from the top down and skip this finishing step. When you do need to stitch knitted pieces together it's important to seam them with this virtually invisible technique. Sewing knitting together is different from stitching fabric; the heavy texture requires that you take the time to carefully line up the stitches to ensure that the finished piece lies flat.

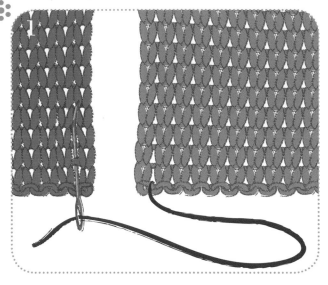

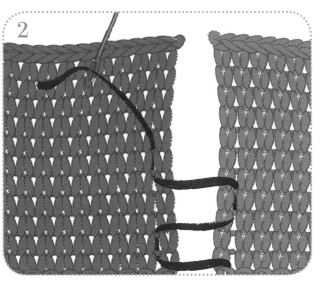

1. ARRANGE PIECES, BEGIN SEAMING

Align the two pieces of knitting as you intend to sew them. Thread a yarn needle onto the tail of one of the pieces or onto a piece of scrap yarn. Bring the needle under the bar between two stitches in the first row.

2. CONTINUE SEAMING

Draw the needle through a second bar between two stitches on the next row up. Bring the needle over to the other piece and draw the needle through two bars on that piece one row up from the row on the other piece. Continue to bring the needle through two bars on each piece, each time beginning one row up.

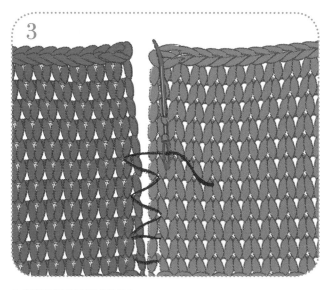

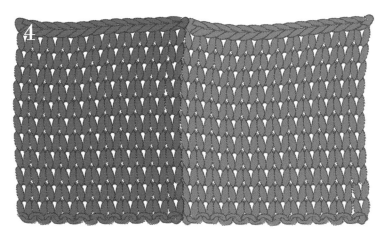

3. TIGHTEN UP SEAM

Continue seaming the pieces together, tightening up the connection after every few stitches.

4. FINISH SEAMING

Once you have seamed the pieces and tightened the yarn, you will have a seamless piece of knitted fabric. Tie off the end and weave in the tail.

When seaming together pieces worked in contrasting colors, use an invisible seaming technique. After picking up two bars directly across from each other, go back into the hole you started from. Move up to the next row and repeat. The additional stitches will hold the pieces closer together and completely conceal the seam.

CROCHETING A CHAIN

Why is there a crocheting technique in a knitting book, you ask? Well, it became necessary, and hey, maybe you might get hooked on a whole new way to work with your yarn. The chain is the first step of any crochet piece, but it's also just like a single knitted stitch that keeps growing with every new loop of yarn. When an I-cord just can't be made small enough, a crochet chain is the perfect solution.

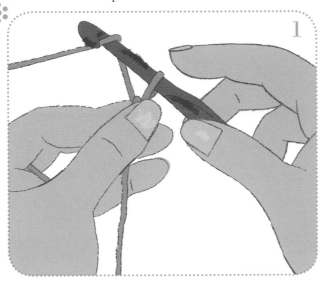

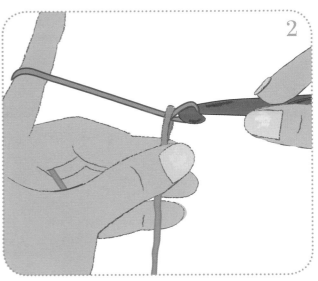

1. MAKE SLIP KNOT AND WRAP YARN FOR FIRST CHAIN

Make a slip knot at the free end of yarn (the other end will be attached to the skein/ball). Slide the slip knot onto a crochet hook, then wrap the working yarn around the back of the hook clockwise.

2. CREATE FIRST CHAIN STITCH

Move the hook so it grabs the wrapped working yarn, and then pull the working yarn through the slip knot to form the first chain stitch.

3. CONTINUE TO MAKE CHAIN

Continue to wrap the working yarn and pull it through each subsequent loop until the chain is the desired length.

THE PATTERNS

IF THIS BOOK HAS FOUND ITS WAY INTO YOUR HANDS, WE ALREADY SHARE A COMMON BOND: A LOVE OF CHILDREN. They bless our days with smiles and make us stop to appreciate the wonder all around. It's not surprising that we want to wrap them in knitted softness or present them with a funny toy, a tangible handcrafted display of our love.

Knitting for children can be fabulously entertaining, especially when you take into account that children are small, hence most kids' knitting projects are small. It's easy and fast to whip up a small-scale zippered vest with a colorful tassel pull (pictured at left, see page 60 for the pattern), a Jackie O-inspired *Swing Jacket* (see page 74) and even a cute-as-pie rollneck sweater with an intarsia giraffe (see page 40) when an adult-size version might take an entire winter.

Kids also love bright colors and soft yarns, and that combo is guaranteed to make you happy while you knit. You won't be able to put down the *Fuzzy Bolero Sweater* made from a super-soft yarn once you get started (see page 86), and the *Pup + Cat Pocket Scarf + Matching Hat Sets* (see page 112) are soft and bright— you won't be able to suppress a giggle as you sew on the button eyes.

Based on hours of professional mama playtime, I created toys that are guaranteed to engage children and not be left on the shelf to collect dust. What toddler can resist a trio of talking animal puppets that can join them in the bathtub (see page 136)? Kindergarteners will love a life-sized floppy cat or dog (pictured at left, see page 64 for the pattern) that are so huggable they're sure to find their way under the bedcovers. The traveling castle with its cast of royal puppets will set the stage for imaginary play wherever you go (see page 102). Older kids will be fascinated with the uniquely bizarre stuffed *Wild Things* (see page 132).

Speed is of the essence, but it's not an advantage if the finished project doesn't appeal to children. At all costs, avoid being the bearer of itchy sweaters that break the child out in a rash, or a tight, high-necked jumper that causes them to protest the second it's pulled over their heads. In the pages that follow you'll find irresistible designs made for real kids. They're guaranteed not to bind, rub or irritate. Knitted with buttery soft yarns in flattering shapes, they'll embrace them like a gentle hug.

On the practical side, I searched for yarns that not only came in wonderful colors but also could be easily laundered. No one wants to see their handiwork ruined after a trip to the park and a stop at the ice cream shop. On a couple of occasions I did waiver from the washable standard because the yarn was just too sumptuous to pass up, and in those cases the garment is an outer layer to help keep it clean.

The patterns that follow are roughly arranged beginning with garments that work best for infants and younger babies, and ending with projects better suited for toddlers and older children. Many of the projects are designed to coordinate, and these items are grouped next to each other. For instance, you can make the *Castle Purse* (see page 102) with scraps left over from the *Striped Vests* (see page 98). And the *Fairy-Tale Dolls* (see page 54) are made with leftover scraps from the *Happily-Ever-After Dress* (pictured below, see page 50 for the pattern).

peek-a-boo Bear stroller blanket

necessity is the mother of invention, and in this case motherhood necessitated the design. Last fall I had the frustrating experience of pushing our muddy stroller wheels over a blanket that I'd just carefully wrapped around my daughter. That's why I made this washable blanket big enough to keep your little one warm but still small enough to avoid interfering with the wheels. Four handy ties attach it to the sides of the stroller and keep it in place. The pocket is a clever diversion for your toddler, who will enjoy both filling it with toys and treasures and promptly emptying it again. If you like, you can make the chubby little bear shown here to peek out of the stroller blanket pocket.

BLANKET

Finished Measurements

24" x 31" (61cm x 79cm)

Yarn

3 skeins Plymouth Yarns Encore Mega Colorspun (acrylic/wool blend, 64 yds [59m] per 100g skein) in color #7129 blues and greens (MC)

1 skein Encore Mega in #2426 purple (CC1)

1 skein Plymouth Yarns Oh My! (nylon, 70 yds [64m] per 50g skein) in #18 blue (CC2)

Needles

24" (61cm) or longer US 15 (10mm) circular needle

1 set of 5 size US 9 (5.5mm) DPNs

Notions

scrap yarn

yarn needle

Gauge

8 sts and 14 rows = 4" (10cm) in St st with larger needle

KNITTING SKILLS

garter st [garter stitch]: Knit every row

I-cord: Knit a tube with 2 DPNs by knitting only one side of the work (see page 17)

k2tog [knit 2 together]: Dec by knitting 2 sts tog as 1 st (see page 14)

kfb [knit 1 front and back]: Inc by knitting 1 in the front and back of the next st (see page 15)

m1 [make 1]: Inc by picking up the bar between 2 sts from front to back, place it on the left-hand needle, then knit it through the back loop (see page 15)

pm [place marker]: Slide a marker onto the needle as indicated

sm [slip marker]: Slide a marker from one needle to the other as indicated

St st [Stockinette stitch]: Knit on right side, purl on wrong side

yo [yarn over]: Wrap the yarn once around the right-hand needle and cont knitting; on the subsequent row, treat the wrap as a st, creating an eyelet hole in the knitted fabric

BLANKET

With CC1 and larger needles, CO 48 sts. Work in garter st for 5 rows.

EYELET ROW for ties (RS): K1, k2tog, yo, knit to last 3 sts, yo, k2tog, k1.

NEXT ROW (WS): K3, purl to last 3 sts, k3.

NEXT ROW (RS): Knit.

Rep last 2 rows twice more. Change to MC. Cont as est, keeping 3 sts at each side in garter st until Blanket measures 27" (69cm), ending with a WS row.

Change to CC1, and work 6 rows even. Rep Eyelet Row. Work 5 rows in garter st. BO.

POCKET

To locate the position of the Pocket, count down sixteen rows from the first CC1 row at the top of the Blanket. Mark this row with a scrap of colored yarn. Then count 18 sts in from either side and mark both of these points with yarn scraps.

With MC, pick up and knit 12 sts between the markers. (See the Glossary on page 155 for instruction on picking up sts.) Work in St st for 13 rows. Work in garter st for 3 rows. Change to CC1 and BO.

Sew sides of Pocket to Blanket.

TIES (MAKE 4)

With smaller needles and CC2, CO 8 sts. Knit 8" (20cm) of I-cord (see page 17 in the Learning the Basics section for step-by-step instructions on knitting I-cord). BO.

FINISHING

Weave in ends. Loop each tie through an eyelet in the Stroller Blanket.

TEDDY BEAR

Finished Measurements

approx 7" (18cm) tall

Yarn

1 skein Plymouth Yarns Oh My! (nylon, 82 yds [75m] per 50g skein) each in color #19 green (MC) and color #18 blue (CC)

Needles

2 size US 9 (5.5mm) circular needles

OR 1 set of 5 size US 9 (5.5mm) DPNs

Notions

polyester fiberfill

stitch holder or scrap yarn

stitch marker

yarn needle

Gauge

14 sts and 20 rows = 4" (10cm) in St st

TEDDY BEAR

This little bear is very huggable and fits perfectly into little arms. He could be a darling gift all on his own, or consider coordinating him with a baby sweater (see the *Rollneck Giraffe Sweater* on page 40) to make an irresistible gift set.

HEAD

With MC, CO 10 sts. Divide evenly over DPNs or over 2 circular needles and join for working in the rnd. (See page 16 in the Learning the Basics section for step-by-step instructions on knitting in the round with 2 circular needles.) Pm at beg of rnd and after 5 sts to indicate the sides of the Head and Body. Knit 1 rnd.

NEXT RND: *K1, m1, knit to 1 st before marker, m1, k1, sm; rep from * once—14 sts.

Rep last 2 rnds 3 times more—26 sts. Knit 2 rnds.

NEXT RND: *K2tog, knit to 2 sts before marker, k2tog, sm; rep from * once—22 sts.

Rep last rnd 3 times more—10 sts.

SHOULDERS

NEXT RND: (M1, knit to end of needle, m1) twice—14 sts.

Knit 1 rnd.

Rep last 2 rnds twice more—22 sts.

ARMHOLES

Divide body into 2 sets of 11 sts each (for front and back) and work separately in rows to make openings for the Arms, adding a second length of yarn to work sts on back.

Work 3 rows.

Rejoin and knit 2 rnds.

TUMMY

NEXT RND: *K1, m1, knit to 1 st before marker, m1, k1, sm; rep from * once—26 sts.

Rep last rnd twice more—34 sts.

LEGS

DIVIDE FOR LEGS: K8, place next 17 sts on holder, knit rem 9 sts—17 sts.

Knit 3 rnds. Pm at inside of Leg, after first 8 sts.

NEXT RND: Knit to marker, sm, k2tog, knit to end—16 sts.

Knit 1 rnd.

NEXT RND: Knit to 2 sts before marker, k2tog, sm, knit to end—15 sts.

Knit 1 rnd.

Rep last 4 rnds once more, then first rnd only once—12 sts.

NEXT RND: K2tog, k4, k2tog, k4—10 sts.

Break yarn, draw through rem sts and fasten off. Replace 17 held sts on needles, join new yarn and work as for first Leg.

ARMS (MAKE 2)

Before knitting the Arms, use the Arm openings to stuff the Bear with fiberfill.

Pick up 12 sts around opening and join for working in the rnd. Knit 4 rnds.

NEXT RND: K2tog, k4, k2tog, k4—10 sts.

Knit 3 rnds.

NEXT RND: K2tog, k3, k2tog, k3—8 sts.

Push stuffing through the open end of the Arm. Break yarn, draw through rem sts and fasten off.

EARS (MAKE 2)

Pick up 5 sts from one side of the top of the Head.

Knit 1 row. Purl 1 row.

NEXT ROW: K2tog, k1, k2tog—3 sts.

BO.

FINISHING

Weave in all the loose ends, using them to help strengthen the Arm and Leg connections. Use CC to make two French knots for eyes, stitch a triangular nose and an elongated "w" for the mouth.

stretchy I-corD Hats

THIS STRETCHY, COMFY HAT MUST BE THE ALL-TIME BEST KNITTED BABY GIFT. Just pick two colors of Cascade Fixation and buy a skein of each to make two hats in no time at all. Soft to the touch and truly elastic, it would take an extremely clever baby to pull off this handsome hat. Newborn outfits are sometimes worn only a few times before they're outgrown, but this everyday essential will surely be appreciated for months to come. And these hats are quick to knit since they're so small.

KNITTING SKILLS

I-cord: Knit a tube with 2 DPNs by knitting only 1 side of the work (see page 17)

k2tog [knit 2 together]: Dec by knitting 2 sts tog as 1 st (see page 14)

St st [Stockinette stitch]: Knit on the right side, purl on the wrong side

Sizes

newborn (6 12 mos, 12–24 mos)

Finished Measurements

Hat circumference: 12 (13½, 16)" [31 (34, 41)cm], unstretched

Yarn

1 skein each Cascade Yarns Fixation (cotton/elastic blend, 100 yds [91m] per 50g skein [measured unstretched]) in color #9349 variegated red (MC1), color #9939 variegated tan (CC1), color #3628 solid red (MC2) and color #7360 solid tan (CC2)

Needles

2 size US 9 (5.5mm) circular needles OR 1 set of 5 size US 9 (5.5mm) DPNs

Notions

yarn needle
stitch marker

Gauge

23 sts and 34 rows = 4" (10cm) in St st

HAT

With CC, CO 70 (78, 92) sts. Divide evenly between the 2 circular needles (or DPNs) and join for working in the rnd, taking care not to twist sts.

Work in St st for 2 (3)" [5 (8)cm]. Change to MC. Cont in St st until Hat measures 5 (5½, 6½)" [13 (14, 17)cm] from cast-on edge, dec 1 st on last rnd for the two larger sizes—70 (77, 91) sts.

NEXT RND: *K5, k2tog; rep from * to end—60 (66, 78) sts.

Knit 1 rnd.

NEXT RND: *K4, k2tog; rep from * to end—50 (55, 65) sts.

Knit 1 rnd.

NEXT RND: *K3, k2tog; rep from * to end—40 (44, 52) sts.

Knit 1 rnd.

NEXT RND: *K2, k2tog; rep from * to end—30 (33, 39) sts.

Knit 1 rnd.

NEXT RND: *K1, k2tog; rep fom * to end—20 (22, 26) sts.

Knit 1 rnd.

NEXT RND: K2tog around—10 (11, 13) sts.

SIZES NEWBORN AND 6–12 MOS ONLY:

NEXT RND: K0 (1), *k2tog; rep from * to end—5 (6) sts.

SIZE 12–24 MOS ONLY:

NEXT RND: K1, *k3tog; rep from * to end—5 sts.

Work in I-cord on rem sts for 3" (8cm). (See page 17 in the Learning the Basics section for step-by-step instructions on knitting I-cord.) Break yarn, draw through sts and fasten off. Tie cord into an overhand knot, flush against top of hat.

Weave in ends.

TIP

Cascade Fixation is one adaptable yarn. Its elasticity allows it to be knitted in a huge range of needle sizes. When you're knitting, be sure not to pull the yarn too tightly or hold it too loosely—give it even tension to ensure the best results.

FRUITY BIBS

These pretty and soft lightweight bibs are comfortable enough for baby to wear all day long. The bibs come in two sizes. Make a bigger bib to protect baby's outfit from light meals of puréed pears and sweet potatoes, or make the drool bib to catch milky spills and gurgles. Bamboo has natural antibacterial properties that will help keep the bibs safe and clean. Just three skeins of different colored yarn make all three bibs.

KNITTING SKILLS

garter st [garter stitch]: Knit every row

intarsia: Work in a 2-color pattern by picking up a new color and twisting it around the other color behind the work (see page 18)

k2tog [knit 2 together]: Dec by knitting 2 sts tog as 1 st (see page 14)

pm [place marker]: Slide a marker onto the needle as indicated

sm [slip marker]: Slide a marker from one needle to the other as indicated

St st [Stockinette stitch]: Knit on right side, purl on wrong side

yo [yarn over]: Wrap the yarn once around the right-hand needle and cont knitting; on the subsequent row, treat the wrap as a st, creating an eyelet hole in the knitted fabric

Finished Measurements

Strawberry and Cherry: approx 8¾" x 7¾" (21cm x 20cm)

Daisy: approx 7½" x 4½" (19cm x 11cm)

Yarn

1 skein of Classic Elite Bam Boo (bamboo, 77 yds [70m] per 50g skein) each in color #4915 Bamboo Leaf (A), color #4919 Flamingo (B) and color #4988 Melon (C)

One skein of each color makes the three-bib set.

Needles

size US 7 (4.5mm) straight needles

Notions

stitch holder
stitch markers
three ⅝" (16mm) buttons
yarn needle

Gauge

18 sts and 31 rows = 4" (10cm) in garter st

TIP
If you're looking for a sturdier bib for older babies, you might consider substituting a stiffer yarn.

Note: When working from charts, be sure to twist yarns together at color changes to prevent gaps. (See page 18 in Learning the Basics for step-by-step instructions on intarsia.)

CHERRY BIB

With yarn C, CO 40 sts. Knit 1 row.

Change to yarn B. Cont in garter st for 18 rows.

NEXT ROW (RS): K15, pm, work Row 1 of Cherry Chart over next 10 sts in St st, pm, k15.

NEXT ROW (WS): K15, sm, work Row 2 of Cherry Chart over next 10 sts in St st, sm, k15.

Cont as set for 14 rows of Cherry Chart.

After completing chart, remove markers.

Cont in garter st for 14 rows.

Change to A. Knit 1 row.

NEXT ROW (WS): K15 and place these sts on holder, BO 10, k15.

NECK TAB

NEXT ROW: Knit to last 2 sts, k2tog.

NEXT ROW: Knit.

Rep last 2 rows 4 times more—10 sts.

BO all sts.

NECK STRAP

Transfer 15 held sts to needle and rejoin yarn at neck edge.

NEXT ROW: Knit.

NEXT ROW: Knit to last 2 sts, k2tog.

Rep last 2 rows 4 times more—10 sts.

Cont in garter st for 9" (23cm).

BUTTONHOLE ROW: K4, yo, k2tog, k4.

Knit 1 row.

K2tog at beg of next 2 rows—8 sts.

BO all sts.

STRAWBERRY BIB

With yarn A, CO 40 sts. Knit 1 row.

Change to yarn C. Cont in garter st for 18 rows.

NEXT ROW (RS): K15, pm, work Row 1 of Strawberry Chart over next 10 sts in St st, pm, k15.

NEXT ROW (WS): K15, sm, work Row 2 of Strawberry Chart over next 10 sts in St st, sm, k15.

Cont as set for 14 rows of Strawberry Chart, keeping center 10 sts in St st.

After completing chart, remove markers.

Cont in garter st for 14 rows.

34

Change to yarn B. Knit 1 row.

NEXT ROW (WS): K15 and place these sts on holder, BO 10, k15.

Work Neck Tab and Strap as for Cherry Bib.

DAISY DROOL BIB

With yarn B, CO 34 sts. Knit 1 row.

Change to yarn A. Cont in garter st for 6 rows.

NEXT ROW (RS): K12, pm, work Row 1 of Daisy Chart over next 10 sts in St st, pm, k12.

NEXT ROW (WS): K12, sm, work Row 2 of Daisy Chart over next 10 sts in St st, sm, k12.

Cont as set for 12 rows of Daisy Chart, keeping center 10 sts in St st.

After completing chart, remove markers.

Cont in garter st for 10 rows.

Change to yarn C. Knit 1 row.

NEXT ROW (WS): K12 and place these sts on holder, BO 10, k12.

NECK TAB

NEXT ROW: Knit to last 2 sts, k2tog.

Knit 1 row.

Rep last 2 rows 3 times more—8 sts.

BO all sts.

NECK STRAP

Transfer 12 held sts to needle and rejoin yarn at neck edge.

NEXT ROW: Knit.

NEXT ROW: Knit to last 2 sts, k2tog.

Rep last 2 rows 3 times more—8 sts.

Cont in garter st for 6" (15cm).

BUTTONHOLE ROW: K3, yo, k2tog, k3.

Knit 1 row.

K2tog at beg of next 2 rows—6 sts.

BO all sts.

FINISHING (ALL)

Weave in ends. Stitch a button to the Neck Tab, aligning it with the buttonhole.

FLAMINGO

MELON

BAMBOO LEAF

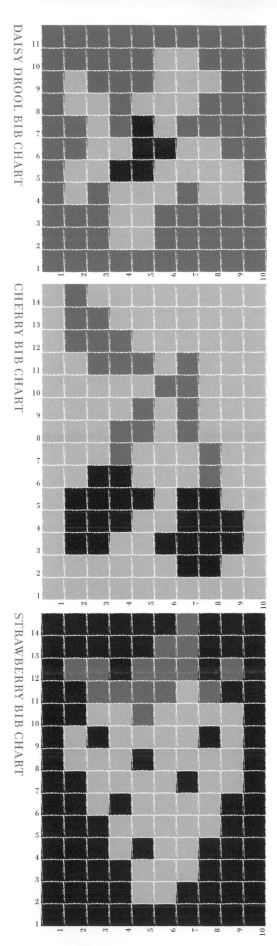

DAISY DROOL BIB CHART

CHERRY BIB CHART

STRAWBERRY BIB CHART

BaBy Hats + MatcHinG MITTS

Mitts pattern by Becka Homan

THESE HATS TRULY EPITOMIZE THE SOFT AND SIMPLE STYLE. The double strand of yarn and muted colors make them irresistible to touch. Both the earflaps and the thickness of the knitting will keep little heads warm all winter long. Who can resist a little boy in this teddy bear hat? Or a sweet little girl in the pink sweetheart version? When you finish the hat, make matching toddler mitts to keep little fingers warm. Just slip them down over their little fists—there's no need to wiggle unwilling thumbs. And the long cuffs help keep the mitts in place. If you're concerned about losing a mitt, connect them to a chain-stitch length and thread it through their coat.

Sizes

12 mos (24 mos)

Finished Measurements

Hat circumference: 16" (41cm)
Mitt circumference: 7" (18cm)

Yarn

BEAR

2 skeins Berroco Chinchilla (rayon, 77 yds [71m] per 50g skein) each in color #5535 Fawn (MC) and in color #5517 Cola (CC)

Turn to page 39 to see the Bear version.

SWEETHEART

2 skeins Berroco Chinchilla each in color #5344 Pink Champagne (MC) and in color #5513 English Rose (CC)

The Sweetheart version is pictured opposite.

KNITTING SKILLS

garter st [garter st]: Knit every row

I-cord: Knit a tube with 2 DPNs by knitting only 1 side of the work (see page 17)

k2tog [knit 2 together]: Dec by knitting 2 sts tog as 1 st (see page 14)

m1 [make 1]: Inc by picking up the bar between 2 sts from front to back, place it on the left-hand needle, then knit it through the back loop (see page 15)

pm [place marker]: Slide a marker onto the needle as indicated

sm [slip marker]: Slide a marker from one needle to the other as indicated

St st [Stockinette stitch]: Knit on right side, purl on wrong side

Needles

2 size US 8 (5mm) circular needles
OR 1 set of 5 size US 8 (5mm) DPNs

Notions

scrap yarn
stitch markers
yarn needle

Gauge

11 sts and 16 rows = 4" (10cm) in St st with 2 strands of yarn held together

BEAR (SWEETHEART) HAT

With 2 strands of CC held together, CO 46 sts (for both sizes). Divide evenly over 2 circular needles or over DPNs and join for working in the rnd, being careful not to twist sts. (See page 16 in the Learning the Basics section for step-by-step instructions on working in the round with 2 circular needles.)

Work in k1, p1 rib for 6 rnds, k2tog on last rnd—45 sts.

Change to MC. Knit 3 rnds.

NEXT RND: *K9, pm; rep from * 4 times more.

DEC RND: *Knit to 2 sts before marker, k2tog, sm; rep from * 4 times more—40 sts.

Knit 3 (4) rnds.

Rep Dec Rnd—35 sts.

Knit 2 (3) rnds.

Rep Dec Rnd—30 sts.

Rep last 3 (4) rnds twice more—20 sts.

Knit 1 (2) rnds.

Rep Dec Rnd—15 sts.

Knit 1 rnd.

BEAR: BO loosely.

SWEETHEART: Rep last 2 rnds twice more—5 sts.

Cut yarn, leaving a 6" (15cm) tail. Draw tail through rem sts, pull tight and fasten off.

EARFLAPS

Using MC (CC), working in first row above ribbing, pick up and knit 10 sts: 5 sts on either side of cast-on tail. (See page 155 in the Glossary for instructions on picking up sts.)

Work 8 rows in garter st.

DEC ROW: K2tog, knit to last 2 sts, k2tog—8 sts.

Knit 3 rows.

Rep Dec Row—6 sts.

Knit 2 rows.

Rep Dec Row—4 sts.

Change to CC (MC). Work I-cord over rem sts for 2" (5cm). (See page 17 in the Learning the Basics section for step-by-step instructions on knitting I-cord.)

Fasten off, leaving a tail of yarn to attach pompom.

Work second Earflap on opposite side of Hat.

EARS (BEAR HAT ONLY)

Fold Hat flat with Earflaps at sides. With CC, pick up and knit 8 sts from one side of top. With a second needle, working directly behind the first set of sts, pick up and knit 8 sts—16 sts.

Join and work in St st in the rnd for 6 rnds.

NEXT RND: K2tog at the bottom of the Ear on each needle—14 sts.

NEXT RND: K2tog at the top of the Ear on each needle—12 sts.

NEXT RND: K2tog, k2, k2tog twice, k2, k2tog—8 sts.

NEXT RND: K2tog around—4 sts.

Break yarn, draw through rem sts and fasten off.

Rep on opposite side of Hat for second Ear.

Once the Ears are complete, sew together the bound-off sts at the top of the Hat.

FINISHING
Weave in ends.

POMPOMS
Create 2" (5cm) pompoms for the Earflaps by wrapping yarn around the thumb and forefinger of your left hand. Continue wrapping until you have approx a 1" (3cm) thick wrap. Remove the wound yarn from your fingers and tightly wrap and knot the center of the loop with scrap yarn. Cut open the loops and then trim the pompom into a round shape. Thread the ends of the yarn scrap onto a yarn needle and sew the pompom to the I-cord. Thread the I-cord tail through the needle and sew it up and down through the pompom to strengthen the connection.

Create a 3½" (9cm) pompom for the top of the Sweetheart Hat using the same technique, except this time wrap the yarn around all four of your fingers and keep wrapping until the loop is over 1" (3cm) thick, tie it with scrap yarn, cut open the loops, then shape it with scissors and sew it to the top of the hat.

❧ MITTS
With 2 strands of CC held together, CO 16 sts. Divide evenly over 2 circular needles or over DPNs and join for working in the rnd, being careful not to twist sts. (See page 16 in the Learning the Basics section for step-by-step instructions on working in the round with 2 circular needles.)

Work in k1, p1 rib for 2" (5cm).

Change to MC and work in St st.

NEXT RND: (K2, m1) 3 times, k4, (m1, k2) 3 times—22 sts.

Work even for 2" (5cm).

NEXT RND: K2, k2tog, (k1, k2tog) twice, k3, k2tog, (k1, k2tog) twice, k1—16 sts.

Work even for 1" (3cm).

NEXT RND: K2tog around—8 sts.

Cut yarn, leaving a 6" (15cm) tail. Draw tail through rem sts and fasten off. Weave in ends.

ROLLneck Giraffe sweater

Pattern co-designed by Chesley Flotten

WHen Babies are really Tiny, THe animals on THeir cloTHes are For our enTerTainmenT. Before they turn one, they become very aware of images around them, most especially animals. That's why taking a little extra time to adorn a sweater with this giraffe will make this sweater one of their most popular wardrobe choices. This design was my favorite partnership with Chesley Flotten, the owner of my local yarn store. She figured out the nuts and bolts of the design, including the clever ribbing, and left me with my favorite job of drawing up the playful giraffe for the color chart.

KNITTING SKILLS

intarsia: Work in a 2-color pattern by picking up a new color and twisting it around the other color behind the work (see page 18)

k2tog [knit two together]: Dec by knitting 2 sts tog as 1 st (see page 14)

m1 [make 1]: Inc by picking up the bar between 2 sts from front to back, place it on the left-hand needle, then knit it through the back loop (see page 15)

p2tog [purl two together]: Dec by purling 2 sts tog as 1 st, just as for k2tog

St st [Stockinette stitch]: Knit on right side, purl on wrong side

Sizes

12 mos (24 mos, 4 yrs)

Finished Measurements

Chest: 22 (24½, 26½)" [56 (62, 67)cm]
Length from shoulder: 10 (11, 12½)" [25 (28, 32)cm]

Yarn

3 (4, 5) skeins Berroco Love it (cotton/acrylic/polyester blend, 120 yds [110m] per 50g skein) in color #3221 Walnut (MC)

1 skein Berroco Love it each in color #3230 Salamander (CC1) and in color #3228 Brownstone (CC2)

Needles

size US 8 (5mm) straight needles
size US 6 (4mm) straight needles
1 set of 5 size US 6 (4mm) DPNs

Notions

stitch holders
yarn needle

Gauge

18 sts and 25 rows = 4" (10cm) in St st with larger needles

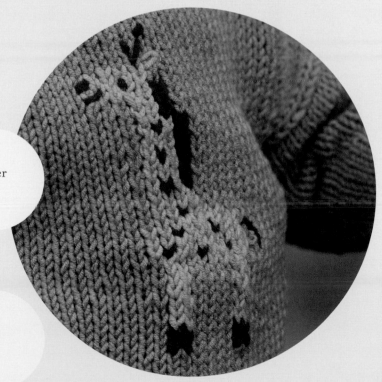

GIRAFFE CHART

(row numbers along left: 1–34; column numbers along bottom: 1–14)

Note: When working chart pattern, twist yarns together at color changes to prevent gaps. (See page 18 in the Learning the Basics section for step-by-step instructions on working in intarsia.)

BACK

With smaller straight needles and MC, CO 52 (57, 62) sts.

ROW 1 (WS): *P2, k1, p1, k1; rep from * to last 2 sts, p2.

ROW 2 (RS): Knit.

Rep Rows 1–2 3 times more.

Change to larger needles and cont in St st (beg with a WS row) until piece measures 9 (10, 11½)" [23 (25, 29)cm], ending with a WS row.

SHAPE NECK AND SHOULDERS

NEXT ROW (RS): K14 (16, 17), place center 24 (25, 28) sts on a holder, join second ball of MC, knit to end.

NEXT ROW (WS): Purl to 2 sts before Neck edge, p2tog; on second Shoulder, p2tog, purl to end.

NEXT ROW: Knit to 2 sts before Neck edge, k2tog; on second Shoulder, k2tog, knit to end—12 (14, 15) sts each Shoulder.

Work even until piece measures 10 (11, 12½)" [25 (28, 32) cm] from cast-on edge. BO all sts.

FRONT

Work as for Back until piece measures 2½ (3, 3½)" [6 (8, 9)cm] from cast-on edge, ending with a WS row.

NEXT ROW (RS): K19 (22, 24), work Row 1 of Giraffe Chart over next 14 sts, k19 (21, 24).

NEXT ROW (WS): P19 (21, 24), work Row 2 of Giraffe Chart over next 14 sts, p19 (22, 24).

Cont as established to end of Chart (30 rows).

Work even until piece measures 9 (10, 11½)" [23 (25, 29)cm] from cast-on edge, ending with a WS row.

Shape Neck and Shoulders as for Back. BO all sts.

SLEEVES (MAKE 2)

With smaller straight needles and MC, CO 32 sts. Work 8 rows of edging as for Back.

Change to larger needles and cont in St st, m1 at each end of first RS row and every foll 4th row 7 (9, 11) times—48 (52, 56) sts.

Work even until Sleeve measures 7 (9, 11)" [18 (23, 28)cm] from cast-on edge. BO all sts.

FINISHING
Join Shoulder seams.

ROLLNECK
Beg at left Shoulder, with RS facing and using MC, with DPNs pick up and knit 5 sts from left side of front Neck, k24 (25, 28) sts from holder, pick up and knit 5 sts from right side of front Neck, pick up and knit 5 sts from right back Neck, k24 (25, 28) sts from holder, pick up and knit 5 sts from left back Neck—68 (70, 76) sts. (See page 155 in the Glossary for instructions on picking up sts.) Join for working in the rnd. Knit 10 rnds. BO loosely.

SEAM SLEEVES TO BODY
Match centers of Sleeve tops to shoulder seams and sew to body. Sew side and Sleeve seams.

ADD EMBROIDERED DETAIL
With CC1 and CC2 tails left from working Chart, embroider details on giraffe: backstitch for nose, mouth, head bumps; French knots for eye and top of bumps; a single chain st loop for ear and three chain st loops for tail.

Weave in ends.

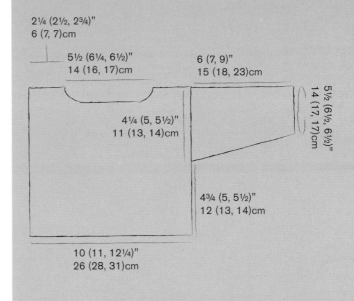

2¼ (2½, 2¾)"
6 (7, 7)cm

5½ (6¼, 6½)"
14 (16, 17)cm

6 (7, 9)"
15 (18, 23)cm

5½ (6½, 6½)"
14 (17, 17)cm

4¼ (5, 5½)"
11 (13, 14)cm

4¾ (5, 5½)"
12 (13, 14)cm

10 (11, 12¼)"
26 (28, 31)cm

COTTON BABY DOLL TOP + MATCHING PURSE

THIS LITTLE TOP WAS INSPIRED BY CELIA'S FAVORITE SUMMER SHIRT. It had a single button closure in the back and flowed loosely around the waist. So comfortable and cool. The colors and texture of this knitted version make the top adaptable for all seasons. Just layer it over a turtleneck or long-sleeved shirt for warmth in cool weather. A perfect project for beginners, it's knitted as a single flat piece from the bottom up. And even embroidering the loop flowers is a breeze. Make use of the leftover yarn along with a single skein of purple to make the matching purse. Perfectly sized for a little girl, the bag is roomy enough to carry a few special treasures, yet still small enough to be easily toted alone. This project is a great way to learn how to pick up stitches around a simple square base. The stitches become the sides of the bag and are knitted in the round all the way to the top edge.

KNITTING SKILLS

est patt [established pattern]: Cont to work in the pattern as it's been established in the previous row/instructions

garter st [garter stitch]: Knit every row

I-cord: Knit a tube with 2 DPNs by knitting only 1 side of the work (see page 17)

k2tog [knit 2 together]: Dec by knitting 2 sts tog as 1 st (see page 14)

pm [place marker]: Slide a marker onto the needle as indicated

sm [slip marker]: Slide a marker from one needle to the other as indicated

St st [Stockinette stitch]: Knit on right side, purl on wrong side

yo [yarn over]: Wrap the yarn once around the right-hand needle and cont knitting; on the subsequent row, treat the wrap as a st, creating an eyelet hole in the knitted fabric

Sizes
12 mos (18 mos, 24 mos, 3–4 yrs, 4–5 yrs, 5–6 yrs)

Finished Measurements
Chest measured at seed st band, unbuttoned). 17 (18, 20, 22, 24, 25½)" [43 (46, 51, 56, 61, 65)cm]

Length: 10½ (11¼, 12¾, 13¼, 14¼, 15¼)" [27 (29, 33, 34, 36, 39)cm]

Purse: approx 7" x 4½" x 4½" (18cm x 12cm x 12cm)

Yarn
1 (1, 1, 2, 2, 3) skein(s) Mission Falls 1824 Cotton (cotton, 84 yds [77m] per 50g skein) each in color #302 Wintergreen (A), in color #406 Lilac (B) and in color #203 Cosmos (C)

small amount of 1824 Cotton in color #206 Peony and in color #204 Lentil for embroidered flowers

leftovers from Baby Doll Top, plus one additional skein of Mission Falls 1824 Cotton in color #406 Lilac for Purse

Needles
16" (41cm) size US 7 (4.5mm) circular needle OR straight needles

16" (41cm) size US 9 (5.5mm) circular needle OR straight needles

Notions
3 ½" (13mm) buttons

stitch holders

stitch markers

yarn needle

Gauge
16 sts and 24 rows = 4" (10cm) in St st with smaller needle

14 sts and 20 rows = 4" (10cm) in St st with larger needle

COTTON BABY DOLL TOP

With yarn A and larger needle, CO 85 (95, 105, 115, 125, 135) sts. Work in garter st for 10 rows. Change to yarn B.

NEXT ROW (RS): (P1, k1) twice, p1, pm, knit to last 5 sts, pm, (p1, k1) twice, p1.

NEXT ROW (WS): (P1, k1) twice, p1, sm, purl to last 5 sts, sm, (p1, k1) twice, p1.

Rep last 2 rows until piece measures 4¾ (5¼, 5¾, 5¾, 6, 6½)" [12 (14, 15, 15, 15, 17)cm] from cast-on edge, ending with a WS row.

Change to smaller needle and yarn C.

NEXT ROW (RS): Work 5 sts in est patt, (k3, k2tog) 15 (17, 19, 21, 23, 25) times, work 5 sts in patt—70 (78, 86, 94, 102, 110) sts.

Work 5 (5, 7, 9, 9, 9) rows even.

NEXT ROW (RS): Work 5 sts in est patt, dec 1 (5, 5, 5, 5, 7) sts evenly spaced over next 60 (68, 76, 84, 92, 100) sts, work last 5 sts in patt—69 (73, 81, 89, 97, 103) sts.

SEED ST EDGING

NEXT ROW (WS): (P1, k1) to last st, p1.

Rep last row once more.

BUTTONHOLE ROW: Work 2 sts in patt, yo, work 2 tog, work in patt to end.

Work 1 more row Seed St.

The next row divides the top of the Baby Doll Top into 2 Straps and a Front.

NEXT ROW (RS): BO 8 (8, 9, 10, 10, 11) sts, work in est patt until there are 6 (6, 7, 7, 9, 9) sts on right-hand needle, then place these sts on a holder, BO 8 (9, 9, 10, 11, 11) sts, work until there are 27 (31, 35, 37) sts on right-hand needle, BO 8 (9, 9, 10) sts, work until there are 6 (6, 7, 7, 9, 9) sts on right-hand needle (after last BO), place these sts on a holder, BO rem sts—27 (31, 35, 37) sts rem on needle.

FRONT PANEL

Note: When changing colors mid-row, be sure to twist yarns together to prevent gaps. (See page 18 in the Learning the Basics section for step-by-step instructions on this technique.)

With RS facing and yarn C, join yarn at armhole edge. Work 4 (5, 6, 7, 7, 8) sts in est Seed St patt, join yarn A and k17 (17, 19, 21, 23, 25) sts, add a second strand of yarn C and work in est Seed St patt to end.

NEXT ROW (WS): Work 4 (5, 6, 7, 7, 8) sts in patt with yarn C, p17 (17, 19, 21, 23, 25) with yarn A, work to end in patt with C.

Cont as est for 4 (6, 8, 10, 12, 14) more rows. Break yarn A and second strand of yarn C.

Work even in Seed St with yarn C until armhole measures 1¾ (1¾, 2¼, 2¾, 3¼, 3¾)" [5 (5, 6, 7, 8, 10)cm], ending with a WS row.

BUTTONHOLE ROW: Work 2 (3, 3, 4, 4, 4) sts, yo, work 2 tog, work to last 4 (5, 5, 6, 6, 6) sts, work 2 tog, yo, work 2 (3, 3, 4, 4, 4) sts.

Work 2 rows even.

Change to yarn B. Knit 1 row. BO all sts.

STRAPS (MAKE 2)

Replace 6 (6, 7, 7, 9, 9) sts from holder on needle. Join yarn C and work in est patt for 5 (5½, 6, 6½, 7¼, 7¾)" [13 (14, 15, 17, 19, 20)cm].

NEXT ROW: K2tog, knit to last 2 sts, k2tog—4 (4, 5, 5, 7, 7) sts.

Rep last row 1 (1, 1, 1, 2, 2) time(s) more—2 (2, 3, 3, 3, 3) sts.

Bind off all sts.

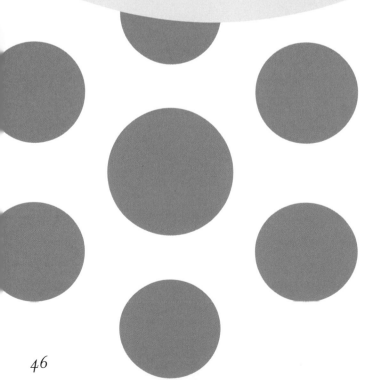

FINISHING

With Peony scraps, embroider 3 lazy-daisy flowers in center Front Panel. Give them French knot centers in Lentil. Use backstitch and chain stitch to make leaves and stems in Lilac.

Sew a button on each strap end, and one on back waistband.

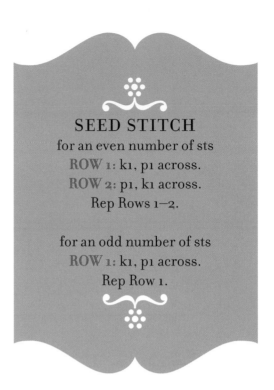

SEED STITCH
for an even number of sts
ROW 1: k1, p1 across.
ROW 2: p1, k1 across.
Rep Rows 1–2.

for an odd number of sts
ROW 1: k1, p1 across.
Rep Row 1.

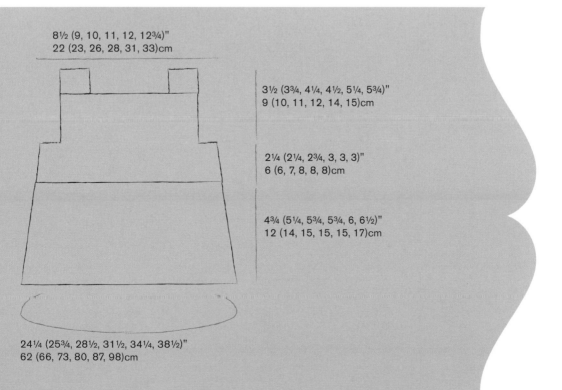

8½ (9, 10, 11, 12, 12¾)"
22 (23, 26, 28, 31, 33)cm

3½ (3¾, 4¼, 4½, 5¼, 5¾)"
9 (10, 11, 12, 14, 15)cm

2¼ (2¼, 2¾, 3, 3, 3)"
6 (6, 7, 8, 8, 8)cm

4¾ (5¼, 5¾, 5¾, 6, 6½)"
12 (14, 15, 15, 15, 17)cm

24¼ (25¾, 28½, 31½, 34¼, 38½)"
62 (66, 73, 80, 87, 98)cm

MATCHING PURSE

With smaller needle and yarn A, CO 20 sts. Work 21 rows in St st, beg with a knit row. Do not turn work at end of last row.

NEXT ROW: Pm, pick up and knit 20 sts from side edge of work, pm, pick up and knit 20 sts from bottom of work (cast-on edge), pm, pick up and knit 20 sts from side edge, pm for beg of rnd—80 sts. (See page 155 in the Glossary for instructions on picking up sts.)

Change to larger needle. Work in garter st for 10 rnds. Change to yarn B. Knit 1 rnd.

NEXT RND: K2tog, *knit to marker, sm, k2tog; rep from * twice, knit to end—76 sts.

NEXT RND: Knit.

Rep last 2 rows 8 times more—48 sts.

Change to smaller needle and yarn C. Knit 2 rnds.

EYELET RND: *BO 1, k5; rep from * to end.

NEXT RND: *Yo, k5; rep from * to end.

Knit 2 rnds.

NEXT RND: *K1, p1; rep from * to end.

NEXT RND: *P1, k1; rep from * to end.

Cont in est seed st pattern for 3 more rnds.

Change to yarn B. Knit 1 rnd. BO all sts.

Weave in ends.

I-cord handle: With larger needle and yarn A, CO 5 sts. Work I-cord for 22" (56cm). (See page 17 in the Learning the Basics section for step-by-step instructions on knitting I-cord.) BO.

Weave the cord through the eyelet holes and tie the ends in a square knot.

Happily-ever-after dress

Pattern by Chesley Flotten

My friend chesley flotten designed this darling dress. The customers in Chesley's Brunswick, Maine, yarn store are always attracted to knitted dress patterns for little girls. When I asked her to consider creating one for this book, she exceeded all my expectations with this sophisticated dress that's buttery soft and comfortable to wear. The full skirt cleverly decreases into a stretchy band that frames the bodice. Destined to be a keepsake, this heirloom dress is simply knit in the round from the bottom up. Don't let your leftover yarn go to waste—transform it into a matching doll (see page 54).

KNITTING SKILLS

k2tog [knit 2 together]: Dec by knitting 2 sts tog as 1 st (see page 15)

p2tog [purl 2 together]: Dec by purling 2 sts tog as 1 st, just as for k2tog

p2tog tbl [purl 2 together through back loop]: With the tip of the right needle, go through the back of the second st on the left needle from left to right, then through the first st on the left needle. Purl the 2 sts tog

pm [place marker]: Slide a marker onto the needle as indicated

sm [slip marker]: Slide a marker from one needle to the other as indicated

ssk [slip, slip, knit]: Slip the first st as if to knit, slip the second st as if to knit, then bring the left needle through both sts from front to back and knit them tog to create a left-leaning dec

St st [Stockinette stitch]: Knit on right side, purl on wrong side

Sizes

9–12 mos (18–24 mos, 3–4 yrs)

Finished Measurements

Chest: 20 (22, 25)" [51 (56, 64)cm]

Length: 16¼ (19¼, 22½)" [41 (49, 57)cm]

Yarn

3 (4, 5) skeins Debbie Bliss Baby Cashmerino (merino wool/microfiber/cashmere blend, 137 yds [125m] per 50g skein in color #010 lilac (MC)

1 (2, 2) skein(s) Debbie Bliss Baby Cashmerino in color #605 lavender (CC)

Needles

24" (60cm) size US 3 (3.25mm) circular needle

1 set of 5 size US 3 (3.25mm) DPNs

16" (41cm) size US 3 (3.25mm) circular needle

Notions

stitch holders

stitch markers

yarn needle

Gauge

25 sts and 32 rows = 4" (10cm) in St st

SKIRT

With circular needle and MC, CO 248 (276, 312) sts. Pm for beg of rnd. Join for working in the rnd, being careful not to twist sts.

RND 1: *K1, p1; rep from * to end.

RND 2: *P1, k1; rep from * to end.

Rep Rnds 1–2 once more.

Cont in St st until Skirt measures 9 (11, 13)" [23 (28, 33)cm] from cast-on edge.

WAISTBAND

RND 1: *K2tog, p2tog; rep from * to end—124 (138, 156) sts.

RND 2: *P1, k1; rep from * to end.

RND 3: *K1, p1; rep from * to end.

Rep Rnds 2–3 until Waistband measures 2" (5cm).

BODICE

Change to CC and work in St st for 1¼ (1¾, 2¼)" [3 (4, 6)cm].

DIVIDE FRONT AND BACK: BO 2 (3, 4) sts, knit until there are 60 (66, 74) sts on right-hand needle. Place rem 62 (69, 78) sts on holder.

You will now be working on the Front and Back separately.

UPPER FRONT

BO 2 (3, 4) sts at beg of next row (WS)—58 (63, 70) sts.

NEXT ROW (RS): Ssk, knit to last 2 sts, k2tog—56 (61, 68) sts.

NEXT ROW: Purl.

Rep last 2 rows 3 (4, 5) times more—50 (53, 58) sts.

Work even until Front measures 3¾ (4½, 5½)" [10 (11, 14)cm] from top of Waistband, ending with a WS row.

NECK SHAPING

ROW 1 (RS): K12 (13, 14), k2tog, place next 22 (23, 26) sts on holder, join second ball of yarn, ssk, k12 (13, 14).

ROW 2 (WS): Purl to 2 sts before Neck edge, p2tog tbl; on second shoulder, p2tog, purl to end—12 (13, 14) sts each side.

Work even on both shoulders until armhole measures 4 (4½, 5¼)" [10 (11, 14)cm]. BO all sts.

UPPER BACK

Replace 62 (69, 78) sts from holder on needle. With RS facing, join yarn. BO 2 (3, 4) sts at beg of next 2 rows—58 (63, 70) sts.

NEXT ROW: Ssk, knit to last 2 sts, k2tog—56 (61, 68) sts.

NEXT ROW: Purl.

Rep last 2 rows 3 (4, 5) times more—50 (53, 58) sts.

Work even until Back measures 4½ (5½, 6¾)" [11 (14, 17)cm] from top of Waistband, ending with a WS row.

NECK SHAPING

ROW 1 (RS): K12 (13, 14), k2tog, place next 22 (23, 26) sts on a holder, join second ball of yarn, ssk, k12 (13, 14).

ROW 2 (WS): Purl to 2 sts before Neck edge, p2tog tbl; on second shoulder, p2tog, purl to end—12 (13, 14) sts each side.

Work even on both shoulders until armhole measures 4 (4½, 5¼)" [10 (11, 13)cm]. BO all sts.

FINISHING
Seam shoulders.

NECK EDGING
With 16" (41cm) circular needle and MC and with RS facing, starting at left shoulder seam, pick up and knit 10 (10, 11) sts down left front Neck edge, k22 (23, 26) sts from holder, pick up and knit 10 (10, 11) sts up right front Neck edge, pick up and knit 6 sts down right back Neck, k22 (23, 26) sts from holder, pick up and knit 6 sts up left back Neck—76 (78, 86) sts. (See page 155 in the Glossary for instructions on picking up sts.)

Pm and join for working in the rnd.

RND 1: *K1, p1; rep from * to end.

RND 2: *P1, k1; rep from * to end.

RND 3: Rep Rnd 1.

BO in pattern.

ARMHOLE EDGING
With DPNs and MC and with RS facing, pick up and knit 50 (56, 64) sts around armhole. BO loosely.

Weave in ends. Block lightly.

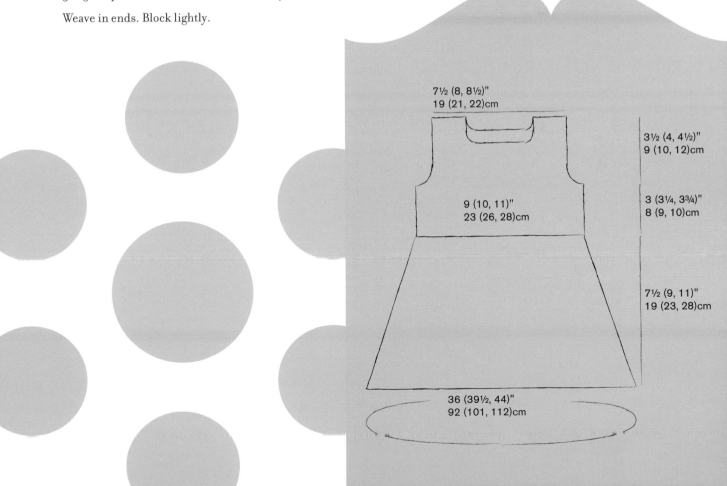

7½ (8, 8½)"
19 (21, 22)cm

3½ (4, 4½)"
9 (10, 12)cm

9 (10, 11)"
23 (26, 28)cm

3 (3¼, 3¾)"
8 (9, 10)cm

7½ (9, 11)"
19 (23, 28)cm

36 (39½, 44)"
92 (101, 112)cm

FAIRY-TALE DOLLS

THESE FLOPPY DOLLS are sure to warm LITTLE HEARTS—THEY'RE SO SOFT YOUR CHILD COULD FALL ASLEEP WITH ONE IN HER ARMS AND NOT BE AWAKENED ALL NIGHT LONG. Her colorful mop of hair reminds me of fairies and mermaids, and its alluring texture begs to be played with. Unlike stiff plastic dolls, her flexible limbs make it very easy for little hands to dress and undress her over and over again. Her wardrobe knits up very quickly so there's no excuse not to make the entire ensemble. Make a pair of these playful dolls with leftovers from the Happily-Ever-After Dress (see page 50).

KNITTING SKILLS

garter st [garter stitch]: Knit every row

k2tog [knit 2 together]: Dec by knitting 2 sts tog as 1 st (see page 14)

m1 [make 1]: Inc by picking up the bar between 2 sts from front to back, place it on the left-hand needle, then knit it through the back loop (see page 15)

St st [Stockinette stitch]: Knit on right side, purl on wrong side

yo [yarn over]: Wrap the yarn once around the right-hand needle and cont knitting; on the subsequent row, treat the wrap as a st, creating an eyelet hole in the knitted fabric

Finished Measurements
approx 12" (30cm) tall

Yarn
1 skein Debbie Bliss Baby Cashmerino (merino wool/microfiber/cashmere blend, 137 yds [125m] per 50g skein) in color #005 light pink OR in color #602 dark pink (MC)

small amounts of Debbie Bliss Baby Cashmerino in color #605 lavender, color #609 purple, color #603 green, color #602 dark pink for faces and clothes

1 skein Online Linie 43 Punta (rayon/nylon/acrylic blend, 90 yds [82m] per 50g skein) in color #29 (light) OR in color #18 (dark) (CC)

Needles
2 size US 5 (3.75mm) circular needles
OR 1 set of 5 size US 5 (3.75mm) DPNs

Notions
crochet hook
polyester fiberfill
stitch holder
yarn needle

Gauge
22 sts and 28 rows = 4" (10cm) in St st with MC

TIP
If you're making a doll to match the Happily-Ever-After Dress, consider knitting it and the clothes on size 3 needles to match the gauge of the dress.

HEAD

With MC, CO 26 sts. Divide evenly over 2 circular needles or over DPNs and join for working in the rnd, taking care not to twist sts. (See page 16 in the Learning the Basics section for step-by-step instructions on working in the round with 2 circular needles.) The beg of the rnd is at the top (or forehead) of the Doll's Head/Body. Work in St st for 10 rnds.

NECK

NEXT RND: *K2tog, k9, k2tog; rep from * once—22 sts.

Knit 1 rnd.

NEXT RND: *K2tog, k7, k2tog; rep from * once—18 sts.

Knit 1 rnd.

NEXT RND: *K2tog, k5, k2tog; rep from * once—14 sts.

Knit 1 rnd.

NEXT RND: *K2tog, k3, k2tog; rep from * once—10 sts.

Knit 4 rnds.

SHOULDERS

NEXT RND: *K1, m1, k3, m1, k1; rep from * once—14 sts.

Knit 1 rnd.

NEXT RND: *K1, m1, k5, m1, k1; rep from * once—18 sts.

Knit 1 rnd.

ARMHOLE

Divide work into 2 sets of 9 sts each, for front and back. Join a second length of yarn for the back and work each set separately for 4 rows.

STOMACH

Rejoin back and front and cont in the rnd for 6 rnds.

HIPS

NEXT RND: *K1, m1, k7, m1, k1; rep from * once—22 sts.

Knit 1 rnd.

NEXT RND: *K1, m1, k9, m1, k1; rep from * once—26 sts.

Knit 1 rnd.

NEXT RND: K1, m1, k13, m1, k12—28 sts.

Work 6 rnds even.

DIVIDE FOR LEGS

K7, place next 14 sts on a holder, knit last 7 sts—14 sts.

LEG

Work 16 rnds even.

NEXT RND: (K2tog, k5) twice—12 sts.

Work 8 rnds even.

NEXT RND: (K2tog, k4) twice—10 sts.

Knit 1 rnd.

FOOT

Change to 1 of the contrast colors. Work 3 rnds even.

NEXT RND: K7, m1, k1, m1, k2—12 sts.

Work 2 rnds even.

NEXT RND: K2tog, k1, k2tog, k7—10 sts.

Knit 1 rnd.

NEXT RND: K5, k2tog, k1, k2tog—8 sts.

Knit 1 rnd.

NEXT RND: K3, k2tog, k1, k2tog—6 sts.

Break yarn, draw through rem sts and fasten off.

Replace 14 sts from holder on needles and work second Leg.

ARMS (MAKE 2)

Use the Armhole openings to stuff the Stomach, Legs and Feet lightly.

With MC, pick up 10 sts around Armhole opening. Divide evenly over DPNs and join for working in the rnd.

Work 10 rnds in St st.

NEXT RND: (K2tog, k3) twice—8 sts.

Work 8 rnds even.

NEXT RND: (K2tog, k2) twice—6 sts.

Knit 1 rnd.

HAND

NEXT RND: (K1, m1) twice, k2, (m1, k1) twice—10 sts.

Work 2 rnds even.

NEXT RND: (K2tog, k3) twice—8 sts.

Knit 1 rnd.

NEXT RND: (K2tog, k2) twice—6 sts.

Knit 1 rnd.

NEXT RND: (K2tog, k1) twice—4 sts.

Break yarn, draw through rem sts and fasten off.

Use the opening in the top of the Head to stuff the Hands, Arms, and chest lightly. Add stuffing to the Neck and Head.

HAIR

With 2 strands of CC held together, pick up and knit 26 sts around cast-on edge of Head. Divide evenly over 2 circular needles or DPNs and join for working in the rnd.

LOOP HAIR: *K1 through back loop (tbl) but do not remove old st from left-hand needle. Knit into front of same st, pull out a long loop of yarn, drop loop, and drop original st from left-hand needle. Rep from * to end. Make loops shorter in front, about 1" (3cm) long, and longer in back, about 4" to 5" (10cm to 13cm).

NEXT RND: K2tog around—13 sts.

NEXT RND: Rep loop rnd, making slightly smaller loops than previous rnd.

NEXT RND: K2tog to last st, k1—7 sts.

NEXT RND: Rep loop rnd, making slightly smaller loops than previous rnd.

NEXT RND: K2tog 3 times, k1—4 sts.

Break yarn, draw through rem sts and fasten off.

FINISHING

Weave in ends, using them to neaten joins at Arms and between Legs as necessary. Embroider face and belly button with doubled strands of contrast colors.

DRESS

The Dress is worked from the top to the hem.

With purple, CO 26 sts. Divide evenly over DPNs and join for working in the rnd, taking care not to twist sts.

Knit 1 rnd, purl 1 rnd, then knit 4 rnds.

EYELET RND: *K2tog, yo; rep from * to end.

Knit 4 rnds.

Next rnd: *K1, m1, k11, m1, k1; rep from * once—30 sts.

Knit 4 rnds.

Join 1 strand of CC and work together with purple yarn. Purl 2 rnds. Break purple yarn and BO in purl with CC.

SHOULDER STRAPS (MAKE 2)

Pick up and knit 4 sts from top of Dress. (See page 155 in the Glossary for instructions on picking up stitches.) Work 9 rows in garter st. BO all sts. Sew bound-off edge to back of dress.

TIE

With dark pink yarn, crochet a chain 12" (30cm) long. (See page 21 in the Learning the Basics section for step-by-step instruction on crocheting a chain.) Thread the chain through the Eyelet Row and tie it in front.

SWEATER

The Sweater is worked from the waist to the neck.

With green, CO 34 sts. Do not join. Work 2 rows in garter st. Cont in St st for 4 rows, beg with a knit row.

ARMHOLES

K6, place rem 28 sts on holder. Work even on these 6 sts for 8 rows. BO.

Replace next 20 sts from holder on needles. With RS facing, join yarn, BO 2 sts, knit to end. Work even on rem 18 sts for 6 rows.

NEXT ROW (WS): BO 5, k8, BO 5—8 sts.

Knit 1 row. BO.

Replace last 8 sts from holder on needles. With RS facing, join yarn, BO 2 sts, knit to end. Work even on these 6 sts for 8 rows. BO.

Sew shoulder seams.

SLEEVES (MAKE 2)

Pick up 14 sts around Armhole. Work in St st in the rnd for 10 rows. Purl 1 rnd. Knit 1 rnd. BO purlwise.

HOT PANTS

Hot Pants are worked from the waist to the hem.

With dark pink, CO 28 sts. Divide evenly over 2 circular needles or over DPNs and join for working in the rnd, taking care not to twist sts. (See page 16 in the Learning the Basics section for step-by-step instructions on working in the round with 2 circular needles.) Work 2 rnds in garter st. Cont in St st for 4 rnds.

DIVIDE LEGS: K7, place next 14 sts on a holder, knit last 7 sts—14 sts.

LEGS

Cont in St st for 16 rnds. Work 4 rnds in garter st. BO.

Replace 14 held sts on needles and complete second Leg as for first Leg.

SKIRT

With green, CO 26 sts. Divide evenly over 2 circular needles or over DPNs and join for working in the rnd, taking care not to twist sts. Work 4 rnds in garter st. Cont in St st for 20 rnds. Work 4 rnds in garter st. BO all sts.

TANK TOP

With lavender, CO 28 sts. Divide evenly over 2 circular needles or over DPNs and join for working in the rnd, taking care not to twist sts. Work 12 rnds in garter st. BO all sts.

FLOWER

With a double strand of purple, embroider a four-petaled flower on the center front of Tank Top. With CC, make a French knot for flower center.

SHOULDER STRAPS

Crochet 2 8" (20cm) chains. (See page 21 in the Learning the Basics section for step-by-step instructions on crocheting a chain.) Thread 1 end of each chain through the top edge from front to back and tie it in a bow.

ZIP-UP Tassel vests

THESE BUTTERY SOFT COTTON VESTS KNIT UP IN A HURRY. Choose from two designs, one with a straightforward cast-on edge, and the other with a stylish longer rib back panel that requires a few additional steps. Both vests call for a front zip closure, but don't be intimidated. I have to admit this was my first experience setting a zipper, and it really is easy. The bright tassel helps little fingers pull the zip closed. Whichever vest design you choose, be sure to knit up the matching stuffed cat or dog toy (see page 64). In my experience, no matter how comfortable the clothing, children always choose toys!

KNITTING SKILLS

k2tog [knit 2 together]: Dec by knitting 2 sts tog as 1 st (see page 14)

m1 [make 1]: Inc by picking up the bar between 2 sts from front to back, place it on the left-hand needle, then knit it through the back loop (see page 15)

St st [Stockinette stitch]: Knit on right side, purl on wrong side

Needles

2 24" (60cm) size US 8 (5mm) circular needles
OR 1 set of 5 size US 8 (5mm) DPNs

Sizes

12–18 mos (24 mos, 3–4 yrs, 5–6 yrs)

Finished Measurements

Chest: 22¼ (24½, 26¾, 29)" [57 (62, 68, 74)cm]

Back length from shoulder: 10 (11¼, 12¼, 13¾)" [25 (29, 31, 35)cm] for curved hem, 10¾ (12, 13, 14½)" [27 (30, 33, 37)cm] for straight hem

Notions

separating zipper
sewing needle and matching thread
yarn needle

Gauge

16 sts and 20 rows = 4" (10cm) in St st

Yarn

CURVED-HEM VEST
2 (3, 3, 3) skeins Blue Sky Alpacas Dyed Cotton (cotton, 150 yds [137m] per 100g skein) in color #617 Lotus (MC)

1 skein Alpacas Dyed Cotton in color #616 Sky (CC)

STRAIGHT VEST
2 (3, 3, 3) skeins Blue Sky Alpacas Dyed Cotton in color #607 Lemongrass (MC)

1 skein Blue Sky Alpacas Dyed Cotton in color #618 Orchid (CC)

CURVED HEM VERSION (PINK & BLUE)

LOWER BODY
With CC and circular needle, CO 35 (38, 41, 44) sts.

ROW 1 (WS): *K2, p1; rep from * to last 2 sts, k2.

ROWS 2–6: Cont in k2, p1 rib, inc 1 st at each end of next 5 rows, working new sts into pattern—45 (48, 51, 54) sts.

ROW 7 (WS): Break yarn. Cast on additional sts for Fronts as follows: Use backwards loop method to CO 22 (25, 28, 31) sts onto right-hand needle, then work in established rib across sts on left-hand needle. (See page 154 in the Glossary for instructions on casting on backward-loop style.) CO 22 (25, 28, 31) sts at end of row—89 (98, 107, 116) sts.

ROW 8 (RS): Work in rib across 24 (27, 30, 33) sts, join MC, k41 (44, 47, 50) with MC, join new length of CC and rib to end.

ROW 9: Rib 23 (26, 29, 32) with CC, p43 (46, 49, 52) with MC, rib to end with CC.

ROW 10: Rib 22 (25, 28, 31) with CC, k45 (48, 51, 54) with MC, rib to end with CC.

ROW 11: Rib 21 (24, 27, 30) with CC, p47 (50, 53, 56) with MC, rib to end with CC.

ROW 12: Rib 20 (23, 26, 29) with CC, k49 (52, 55, 58) with MC, rib to end with CC.

ROW 13: Rib 19 (22, 25, 28) with CC, p51 (54, 57, 60) with MC, rib to end with CC.

Break CC. Cont in St st with MC only across all sts until back measures 5½ (6¼, 6¼, 7¼)" [14 (16, 16, 18) cm] from cast-on edge, ending with a WS row.

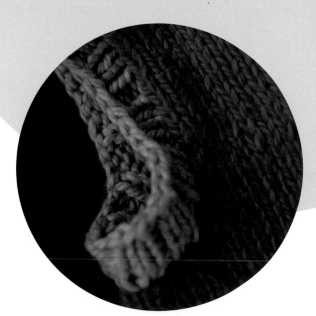

**SHAPE ARMHOLES

NEXT ROW (RS): K20 (22, 24, 26) BO 9, knit until there are 31 (36, 41, 46) sts on right-hand needle, BO 9, knit to end.

UPPER LEFT FRONT
Note: Work each section directly off the circular needles, pushing the sts not in use onto the cord between the 2 needles.

Purl 1 WS row—20 (22, 24, 26) sts.

NEXT ROW: K2tog, knit to end—19 (21, 23, 25) sts.

Rep last 2 rows once more—18 (20, 22, 24) sts.

Work even until Armhole measures 2½ (3, 3½, 4)" [6 (8, 9, 10)cm], ending with a RS row.

SHAPE NECK (WS): BO 6 (7, 8, 9), purl to end—12 (13, 14, 15) sts.

NEXT ROW (RS): Knit to last 2 sts, k2tog—11 (12, 13, 14) sts.

Purl 1 row.

Rep last 2 rows 2 (2, 1, 1) times more—9 (10, 12, 13) sts.

Work even until Armhole measures 4½ (5, 6, 6½)" [11 (13, 15, 17)cm].

BO all sts.

UPPER RIGHT FRONT
Rejoin yarn with WS facing. Purl 1 row.

NEXT ROW (RS): Knit to last 2 sts, k2tog—19 (21, 23, 25) sts.

Rep last 2 rows once more—18 (20, 22, 24) sts.

Work even until Armhole measures 2½ (3, 3½, 4)" [6 (8, 9, 10)cm], ending with a WS row.

SHAPE NECK (RS): BO 6 (7, 8, 9), knit to end—12 (13, 14, 15) sts.

Purl 1 row.

NEXT ROW (RS): K2tog, knit to last 2 sts—11 (12, 13, 14) sts.

Rep last 2 rows 2 (2, 1, 1) times more—9 (10, 12, 13) sts.

Work even until Armhole measures 4½ (5, 6, 6½)" [11 (13, 15, 17)cm]. BO all sts.

UPPER BACK

Rejoin yarn with WS facing. Dec 1 st at beg of next 4 rows—27 (32, 37, 42) sts.

Work even until Armhole measures 4 (4½, 5½, 6)" [10 (11, 14, 15) cm], ending with a WS row.

SHAPE NECK (RS): K9 (10, 12, 13), join a separate length of MC, BO 9 (12, 13, 16) sts , knit to end.

Working each Shoulder separately, work 2 rows even. BO all sts.

FINISHING

Seam shoulders.

ARMHOLE EDGING: With CC and DPNs, RS facing and beg at underarm, pick up and knit 36 (39, 45, 51) sts around Armhole.

Work 4 rnds in k2, p1 rib. BO all sts.

NECK EDGING: With CC and circular needle, RS facing, pick up and knit 13 (15, 17, 18) sts across right front Neck, 15 (17, 19, 20) sts across back Neck, and 13 (15, 17, 18) sts across left front Neck—41 (47, 53, 56) sts. (See page 155 in the Glossary for instructions on picking up sts.)

Work in k2, p1 rib for 4 rows. BO all sts.

FINISHING

ZIPPER

So easy! Don't be intimidated. Place the closed zipper behind the right side of your knitting, so the nylon closure is just barely visible. Pin it in place. With needle and thread, hand stitch the knitted edge to the zipper tape from the right side. If you like, you may slip stitch the free edge of the zipper tape invisibly to the inside of the vest for added neatness and security.

Note: Finish the Vest before buying the zipper. For best results, lay the Vest on a flat surface when measuring the front edges, being careful not to stretch the material. If you can't get a separating zipper in the correct length, buy a longer one and shorten it from the top end. Finish the top of the cut zipper by wrapping thread around the top teeth to stop the zipper from coming off the top.

TASSEL

Make a 2½" (6cm) tassel, using CC for the tassel and MC to tie it off and attach it to the zipper pull. To make the tassel, wrap yarn around 4 fingers of your left hand until the wrapped yarn is ½" (1cm) thick on all sides. Draw 4 double strands of yarn under the loops against your index finger. These strands will later connect to the zipper pull. Carefully remove the tassel from your fingers. Pinch the top and wrap tightly with another strand, knot the ends, and trim. Trim the bottoms off the loops to the desired length.

STRAIGHT HEM VARIATION

With CC, CO 89 (98, 107, 116) sts.

ROW 1: *K2, p1; rep from * to last 2 sts, k2.

Cont in k2, p1 rib for 4 more rows. Change to MC. Work even in St st until piece measures 6¼ (7, 7, 8)" [16 (18, 18, 20)cm] from cast-on edge, ending with a WS row.

Cont as for Curved Hem Version from **.

WHO CAN RESIST THESE BRIGHTLY COLORED FLOPPY CREATURES? Their perfectly squeezable flat bodies are just the right size and shape for pint-sized hugs. No matter how they're positioned, their expressive faces flop up or down to meet your child's gaze. Be sure to knit a matching cuddly vest (see page 60) to keep the practical parents happy.

Finished Measurements

Approx 17½" (44cm) long, from nose to end of tail

Yarn

CAT
1 skein each Blue Sky Alpacas Dyed Cotton (cotton, 150 yds [137m] per 100g skein) in color #617 Lotus (MC) and color #616 Sky (CC)

DOG
1 skein each Blue Sky Alpacas Dyed Cotton (cotton, 150 yds [137m] per 100g skein) in color #618 Orchid (MC) and color #607 Lemongrass (CC)

Needles

1 set of 5 size US 8 (5mm) DPNs
OR 2 size US 8 (5mm) circular needles

Notions

crochet hook
polyester fiberfill
stitch markers
yarn needle

Gauge

16 sts and 20 rows = 4" (10cm) in St st

KNITTING SKILLS

k2tog [knit two together]: Dec by knitting 2 sts tog as 1 st (see page 14)

m1 [make 1]: Inc by picking up the bar between 2 sts from front to back, place it on the left-hand needle, then knit it through the back loop (see page 15)

p2tog [purl two together]: Dec by purling 2 sts tog as 1 st

pm [place marker]: Slide a marker onto the needle as indicated

sm [slip marker]: Slide a marker from one needle to the other as indicated

St st [Stockinette stitch]: Knit on right side, purl on wrong side; when working in the rnd, knit every row

STRIPE PATTERN (CAT ONLY)

Alternate 5 rnds MC with 5 rnds CC. Do not break yarns, but carry up inside work between stripes.

CAT (DOG)

The animals are made from the bottom working up to the Neck; the Tail, Head and Legs are added at the end.

With MC, CO 50 sts. Divide evenly over circular needles (or over DPNs). Join for working in the rnd, being careful not to twist sts, and pm for beg of rnd (center of Belly). (See page 16 in the Learning the Basics section for step-by-step instructions on working in the round with 2 circular needles.)

Knit 5 rnds.

BACK LEG OPENINGS

NEXT RND: K10, BO 5, k20, BO 5, k10—40 sts.

Work the 20 sts of front and back separately in St st for 3 rows, joining a second length of yarn for the back.

NEXT RND (BEG AT MARKER): K10, CO 5 over Leg Opening, k20 from back, CO 5, k10—50 sts. (See page 154 in the Glossary for instructions on casting on backward-loop style.)

BELLY

Work even for 16 (20) rnds.

For the optional intarsia spot on the Dog's back, divide the Body in half, working the back and front separately (knit on RS, purl on WS). Any size or shape of spot works—mine spans 19 rows and starts with 4 sts. The widest part of the spot is 16 sts, and at the end it narrows to 5 sts. (See page 18 in the Learning the Basics section for step-by-step illustrated instructions on working in intarsia.)

CHEST SHAPING (CAT ONLY; DOG, SKIP TO FRONT LEG OPENINGS)

NEXT RND: K1, k2tog, knit to 3 sts before marker, k2tog, k1—48 sts.

Knit 1 rnd.

Rep last 2 rnds once more—46 sts.

FRONT LEG OPENINGS

NEXT RND: K8 (10), BO 5, k20, BO 5, k8 (10)—36 (40) sts.

Work back and front separately for 3 rows, as for Back Leg Openings.

NEXT RND (BEG AT MARKER): K8 (10), CO 5 over Leg Opening, k20 from back, CO 5 over Leg Opening, k8 (10)—46 (50) sts.

NECK SHAPING

NEXT RND: K2, k2tog, knit to 4 sts before marker, k2tog, k2—44 (48) sts.

Knit 1 rnd.

Rep last 2 rnds 7 (9) times more—30 (30) sts.

BO all sts.

BACK LEGS (MAKE 2)

With CC, pick up and k16 sts around Leg Opening. Join for working in the rnd.

Knit 26 (30) rnds.

PAWS

Change to MC.

NEXT RND: (P8, m1) twice—18 sts.

Purl 5 rnds.

NEXT RND: (P2tog, p7) twice—16 sts.

NEXT RND: (P2tog, p6) twice—14 sts.

NEXT RND: (P2tog, p5) twice—12 sts.

BO all sts.

FRONT LEGS (MAKE 2)

With CC, pick up and knit 14 (16) sts around Leg Opening. Join for working in the rnd.

Knit 20 (26) rnds.

PAWS

Change to MC.

NEXT RND: (P7 [8], m1) twice—16 (18) sts.

Purl 5 rnds.

NEXT RND: (P2tog, p6 [7]) twice—14 (16) sts.

NEXT RND: (P2tog, p5 [6]) twice—12 (14) sts.

NEXT RND: (P2tog, p4 [5]) twice—10 (12) sts.

BO all sts.

HEAD

With MC (CC), CO 40 sts. Divide evenly over circular needles (or DPNs) and join for working in the rnd. You're starting at the top of the Head and working down to the chin. Pm at beg of rnd and place another marker after 20 sts; these mark the sides of the Head.

Knit 5 (10) rnds.

DEC RND: *K1, k2tog, knit to 3 sts before marker, k2tog, k1, sm; rep from * once—36 sts.

Knit 3 rnds.

Rep last 4 rnds twice more—28 sts.

Rep Dec Rnd 5 times—8 sts rem.

NEXT RND: K2tog around—4 sts.

Break yarn, draw through rem sts and fasten off.

CAT EARS (MAKE 2)

With MC, pick up 9 sts from top left of front of Head. With circular needle (or a second DPN), pick up 9 sts directly behind these sts, on back side of Head—18 sts. (See page 155 in the Glossary for instructions on picking up sts.) Divide evenly over DPNs and join for working in the rnd. Beg of rnd is at right (inner) edge of Ear.

Knit 5 rnds.

SHAPE OUTSIDE OF EARS

NEXT RND: K6, k2tog, k2, k2tog, knit to end—16 sts.

Knit 1 rnd.

NEXT RND: K5, k2tog, k2, k2tog, knit to end—14 sts.

Knit 1 rnd.

SHAPE OUTSIDE AND INSIDE OF EARS

NEXT RND: (K1, k2tog) twice, k2, (k2tog, k1) twice—10 sts.

NEXT RND: (K2, k2tog, k1) twice—8 sts.

NEXT RND: K2tog twice, BO first st on right-hand needle over second, *k2tog, BO first st over second; rep from * to end. Fasten off.

When making second Ear, pick up sts from back of Head first, then front of Head, so beg of rnd is at left (inner) edge of Ear and outside/inside shaping will remain correct.

DOG EARS (MAKE 2)

With MC, pick up 7 sts from front and back edges of left side of Head (see Cat instructions)—14 sts. Divide evenly over DPNs and join for working in the rnd. Beg of rnd is at right (inner) edge of Ear.

Knit 3 rnds.

BEGIN WIDENING OUTER EDGE OF EAR

NEXT RND: K6, m1, k2, m1, k6—16 sts.

Knit 3 rnds.

NEXT RND: K7, m1, k2, m1, k7—18 sts.

Knit 3 rnds.

NEXT RND: K8, m1, k2, m1, k8—20 sts.

Knit 3 rnds.

NEXT RND: K9, m1, k2, m1, k9—22 sts.

Knit 3 rnds.

NEXT RND: K10, m1, k2, m1, k10—24 sts.

Knit 1 rnd.

SHAPE INSIDE OF EAR

NEXT RND: K1, k2tog, knit to last 3 sts, k2tog, k1—22 sts.

Knit 1 rnd.

NEXT RND: K1, k2tog, knit to last 3 sts, k2tog, k1—20 sts.

SHAPE INSIDE AND OUTSIDE OF EAR

NEXT RND: K1, k2tog, k4, k2tog, k2, k2tog, k4, k2tog, k1—16 sts.

NEXT RND: K1, k2tog, k2, k2tog, k2, k2tog, k2, k2tog, k1—12 sts.

NEXT RND: K1, k2tog twice, k2, k2tog twice, k1—8 sts.

NEXT RND: K2tog twice, BO first st on right-hand needle over second st, *k2tog, BO first st over second; rep from * to end.

Fasten off.

When making second Ear, pick up sts from back of Head first, then front of Head, so beg of rnd is at left (inner) edge of Ear and outside/inside shaping will remain correct.

TAIL

With MC, pick up 6 sts from center of cast-on edge of Belly and 6 sts from center of cast-on edge of Back—12 sts. Divide evenly over 2 circular needles or over DPNs and join for working in the rnd.

For Cat, follow Stripe Pattern as for Body as you knit 35 rnds.

For Dog, knit 18 rnds, change to CC, then knit 17 rnds.

SHAPE END OF TAIL

NEXT RND: (K1, k2tog) 4 times—8 sts.

Knit 1 rnd.

NEXT RND: K2tog twice, BO first st on right-hand needle over second st, *k2tog, BO first st over second; rep from * to end.

Fasten off.

FINISHING

Stuff through the Neck, bottom of Body, and Paw openings. Stitch the Neck, Paws, and bottom edges closed. Stuff the Head, leaving the Ears empty, then stitch the top of the Head closed. Working at the back of the Cat's Head, position the Cat's Neck 3" [8cm] up from the chin and then stitch it in place. Do the same for the Dog, positioning the Neck slightly higher at 3¼" (8cm) from its chin.

With CC (MC), embroider the face. The eyes are made like a large French knot: wrap the yarn 10 times around the needle, pull it up carefully, and then spiral the coiled yarn into a circle, anchoring it in place with a couple more stitches. To make the nose, make five horizontal sts and then cover them with satin stitch worked vertically. The mouth is made with a series of chain stitches.

Tie-on asymmetrical sweater

THIS MUST HAVE BEEN THE BIGGEST DESIGN CHALLENGE IN THE BOOK, BUT THE RESULT IS FANTASTIC. On the practical side, it's easy to knit, comfortable and washable. What makes it unique are the asymmetrical fronts, one of which is knitted from side to side so the variegated yarn stripes run top to bottom. This sweater is warmer than a ballet wrap and has a larger neckline than a kimono, but successfully pulls together the best features of each. The I-cord loops and ties are both decorative and functional. For a quick fasten, just tie them in a loose knot, and for fancier occasions, tie them in little bows.

KNITTING SKILLS

garter st [garter stitch]: Knit every row

I-cord: Knit a tube with 2 DPNs by knitting only 1 side of the work (see page 17)

k2tog [knit 2 together]: Dec by knitting 2 sts tog as 1 st (see page 14)

m1 [make 1]: Inc by picking up the bar between 2 sts from front to back, place it on the left-hand needle, then knit it through the back loop (see page 15)

p2tog [purl 2 together]: Dec by purling 2 sts tog as 1 st, just as for k2tog

St st [Stockinette stitch]: Knit on right side, purl on wrong side

Sizes
6 mos (12 mos, 18–24 mos, 2–3 yrs, 4–5 yrs, 6 yrs)

Finished Measurements
Chest: 20 (22, 24, 26, 28, 30)" [51 (56, 61, 66, 71, 76)cm]
Length: 9 (10½, 12, 13, 13½, 14½)" [23 (27, 30, 33, 34, 37)cm]

Yarn
1 (2, 3, 3, 4, 4) skein(s) Lorna's Laces Shepherd Worsted (superwash wool, 225 yds [206m] per 113g skein) in Bittersweet

Needles
size US 7 (4.5mm) straight needles
1 set of 5 size US 7 (4.5mm) DPNs

Notions
crochet hook
stitch holder
yarn needle
1 ¾" (19mm) button
2 ½" (13mm) buttons

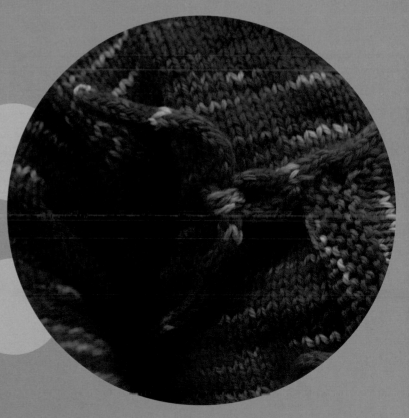

Gauge
18 sts and 24 rows = 4" (10cm) in St st

BACK

CO 44 (50, 54, 59, 63, 68) sts. Work 6 rows in garter st. Work in St st until piece measures 8¼ (9¾, 11¼, 12¼, 12¾, 13½)" [21 (25, 29, 31, 33, 34)cm] from cast-on edge, ending with a WS row.

SHAPE NECK AND SHOULDERS

NEXT ROW (RS): K14 (16, 17, 18, 19, 21), BO 16 (18, 20, 23, 25, 26) sts, knit to end. Leave the first 14 sts on the needles as you knit the Left Shoulder.

LEFT SHOULDER

NEXT ROW: Purl.

NEXT ROW (RS): K2tog, knit to end.

Rep last 2 rows once more—12 (14, 15, 16, 17, 19) sts.

Purl 1 row. BO.

RIGHT SHOULDER

Rejoin yarn at neck edge and purl 1 WS row.

NEXT ROW (RS): Knit to last 2 sts, k2tog.

Rep last 2 rows once more—12 (14, 15, 16, 17, 19) sts.

Purl 1 row. BO.

RIGHT FRONT

CO 27 (30, 32, 35, 38, 40) sts. Work 6 rows in garter st.

NEXT ROW (RS): Knit.

NEXT ROW (WS): Purl to last 4 sts, k4.

Cont as est, keeping 4 sts at center front edge in garter st, until piece measures 5 (6, 7, 7½, 7½, 8)" [13 (15, 18, 19, 19, 20)cm] from cast-on edge, ending with a WS row.

SHAPE NECK

NEXT ROW (RS): K2tog, knit to end—26 (29, 31, 34, 37, 39) sts.

NEXT ROW (WS): Purl to last 2 sts, p2tog—25 (28, 30, 33, 36, 38) sts.

Rep last 2 rows 3 (3, 3, 5, 5, 5) times more—19 (22, 24, 23, 26, 28) sts.

NEXT ROW (RS): K2tog, knit to end—18 (21, 23, 22, 25, 27) sts.

NEXT ROW: Purl.

Rep last 2 rows 6 (7, 8, 6, 8, 8) times more—12 (14, 15, 16, 17, 19) sts.

Work even in St st until Front measures same as Back to Shoulder. BO.

LEFT FRONT

CO 26 (30, 34, 36, 37, 39) sts. Work 6 rows in garter st.

NEXT ROW (RS): Knit to last st, m1, k1—27 (31, 35, 37, 38, 39) sts.

NEXT ROW (WS): Purl to last 4 sts, k4.

Rep last 2 rows 13 (16, 19, 21, 23, 26) times more—40 (47, 54, 58, 61, 65) sts.

Work even, keeping 4 sts at waist edge in garter st, for 2¾ (3, 3¼, 3½, 3¾, 4¼)" [7 (8, 8, 9, 10, 11)cm]. BO.

SLEEVES (MAKE 2)

CO 27 (30, 31, 34, 34, 36). Work 6 rows in garter st.

Change to St st. Inc 1 st at each end of next row and every foll 6th row a total of 5 (5, 7, 8, 10, 11) times—37 (40, 45, 50, 54, 58) sts.

Work even until Sleeve measures 6½ (7½, 9, 10, 10½, 11½)" [17 (19, 23, 25, 27, 29)cm] from cast-on edge. BO.

FINISHING

Seam Shoulders. Mark center of each Sleeve top, match to Shoulder seam, and join to Body. Sew side and Sleeve seams.

COLLAR AND LOOPS

With DPNs, CO 4 sts. Work I-cord for about 24 (27, 30, 33, 36, 39)" [61 (69, 76, 84, 91, 99)cm]. (See page 17 in the Learning the Basics section for step-by-step instructions on knitting I-cord. Place sts on holder.)

Pinch the cast-on end of I-cord into a 2½" (6cm) loop. Starting at Left Front Neck edge, stitch the loop to the Sweater. Cont stitching I-cord into place all around Neckline. Rip back any excess so that I-cord ends flush with Right Front Edge. Fasten off, leaving an 8" (20cm) tail. With tail, crochet a chain 1½" (4cm) long. (See page 21 in the Learning the Basics section for step-by-step instructions on crocheting a chain.) Form chain into a button loop and stitch it in place.

Knit a second length of I-cord, enough to make another 2½" (6cm) loop. Stitch it in place on the Left Front, about 4" (10cm) below first loop.

TIES

Make 2 10" (25cm) lengths of I-cord. Stitch the centers of the Ties to the Right Front of the Sweater, making sure Ties line up with loops on Left Front. Use 2 small buttons on WS of Sweater to anchor ties.

Stitch the third button to WS of Left Front, lining it up with the button loop on Right Front Neck.

Weave in ends.

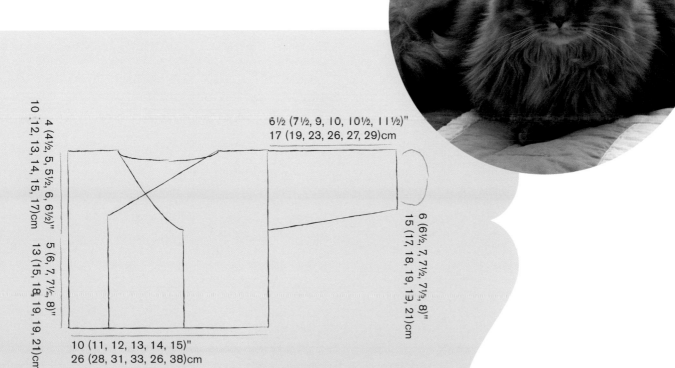

6½ (7½, 9, 10, 10½, 11½)"
17 (19, 23, 26, 27, 29)cm

4 (4½, 5, 5½, 6, 6½)"
10 (12, 13, 14, 15, 17)cm

5 (6, 7, 7½, 8)"
13 (15, 18, 19, 19, 21)cm

6 (6½, 7, 7½, 7½, 8)"
15 (17, 18, 19, 19, 21)cm

10 (11, 12, 13, 14, 15)"
26 (28, 31, 33, 26, 38)cm

swing Jacket

Pattern by Chesley Flotten

Perfect for the little princess in your life, this flouncy sweater jacket will follow her every spin and jump with a swish of color. A stylish cover-up for any girly outfit, this jacket won't cinch in billowy tops or dresses. Soft, luxurious Malabrigo yarn is an absolute joy to knit with, and the worsted weight is warm enough to take the chill out of a crisp autumn or damp spring day. This clever pattern worked from the top down with no seams (it requires almost no finishing!) is graciously provided by Chesley Flotten. My deep gratitude to her for helping turn my idea into a knitted reality.

Sizes

12 mos (24 mos, 3–4 yrs, 5–6 yrs)

Finished Measurements

Chest: 22 (25, 28, 31)" [56 (64, 71, 79)cm]
Length: 12 (14, 18, 22)" [30 (36, 46, 56)cm]

Yarn

2 (2, 3, 5) skeins Malabrigo Merino Worsted (merino wool, 215 yds [197m] per 100g skein), in color #157 Amoroso

Needles

24" (60cm) size US 8 (5mm) circular needle
1 set of 5 size US 8 (5mm) DPNs

Notions

scrap yarn
stitch markers
yarn needle

Gauge

16 sts and 24 rows = 4" (10cm) in St st

KNITTING SKILLS

garter st [garter st]: Knit every row

I-cord: Knit a tube with 2 DPNs by knitting only 1 side of the work (see page 17)

k2tog [knit 2 together]: Dec by knitting 2 sts tog as 1 st (see page 14)

kfb [knit 1 front and back]: Inc by knitting 1 into the front and back of the next st (see page 15)

m1 [make 1]: Inc by picking up the bar between 2 sts from front to back, place it on the left-hand needle, then knit it through the back loop (see page 15)

pm [place marker]: Slide a marker onto the needle as indicated

sm [slip marker]: Slide a marker from one needle to the other as indicated

ssk [slip, slip, knit]: Sl the first st as if to knit, slip the second st as if to knit, then bring the left needle through both sts from front to back and knit them tog to create a left-leaning dec

St st [Stockinette stitch]: Knit on right side, purl on wrong side

YOKE

The Jacket is knit in one piece from the neck down.

With circular needle, CO 2 sts, pm, CO 10 (10, 12, 14) sts, pm, CO 14 (14, 19, 23) sts, pm, CO 10 (10, 12, 14) sts, pm, CO 2 sts—38 (38, 47, 55) sts.

ROW 1 (RS): Kfb twice, sm, kfb, *knit to 1 st before marker, kfb, sm, kfb; rep from * twice, kfb in last st—48 (48, 57, 65) sts.

ROW 2 (WS): Purl.

ROW 3: K1, m1, *knit to 1 st before marker, kfb, sm, kfb; rep from * 3 times, knit to last st, m1, k1—58 (58, 67, 75) sts.

ROW 4: Purl.

ROW 5: *Knit to 1 st before marker, kfb, sm, kfb; rep from * 3 times, knit to end—66 (66, 75, 83) sts.

ROW 6: Purl.

SIZES 12 AND 24 MOS:
Rep Rows 3–6 4 times more, until there are 36 sts between the markers—138 sts.

SIZE 3–4:
Rep Rows 3–6 2 times more, then Rows 3–4 3 times more—141 sts.

SIZE 5–6:
Rep Rows 3–6 2 times more, then Rows 3–4 5 times more—169 sts.

ALL SIZES

NEXT ROW (RS): *Knit to 1 st before marker, kfb, sm, kfb; rep from * 3 times, knit to end—146 (146, 149, 177) sts.

NEXT ROW (WS): K4, purl to last 4 sts, k4.

Rep last 2 rows 3 (5, 6, 5) times more—153 (176, 197, 217) sts.

DIVIDE SLEEVES FROM BODY

NEXT ROW (RS): Knit to first marker, remove marker, k1, place all rem sts to second marker on a piece of scrap yarn, remove second marker, CO 2 onto tip of right needle, pm, CO 2. Knit to third marker, remove marker, k1, place all rem sts to fourth marker on a piece of scrap yarn, remove fourth marker, CO 2, pm, CO 2. Knit to end. There are 89 (108, 113, 125) sts on the needle.

Note: The very first st of each Sleeve is knit with the Body of the Sweater and the rest of the sts become the Sleeve. That keeps the raglan line with the Body, instead of pulling it in with the Sleeve.

BODY

NEXT ROW AND ALL WS ROWS: K4, purl to last 4 sts, k4.

NEXT ROW (RS): Knit to 1 st before marker, m1, k1, sm, k1, m1, k20 (24, 26, 29), m1, pm, k3, pm, m1, knit to 1 st before marker, m1, k1, sm, k1, m1, knit to end.

Work 1 WS row.

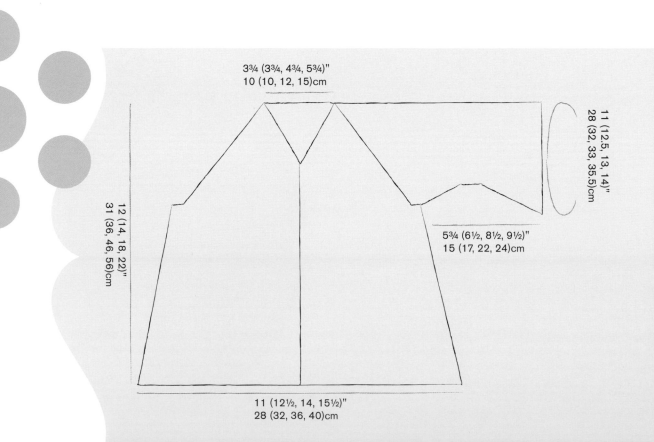

3¾ (3¾, 4¾, 5¾)"
10 (10, 12, 15)cm

11 (12.5, 13, 14)"
28 (32, 33, 35.5)cm

12 (14, 18, 22)"
31 (36, 46, 56)cm

5¾ (6½, 8½, 9½)"
15 (17, 22, 24)cm

11 (12½, 14, 15½)"
28 (32, 36, 40)cm

INC ROW (RS): Knit to 1 st before marker, m1, k1, sm, k1, m1, knit to marker, m1, sm, k3, sm, m1, knit to 1 st before marker, m1, k1, sm, k1, m1, knit to end.

Cont in St st, keeping 4 sts at each front edge in garter st, and rep Inc Row on every 4th (4th, 6th, 8th) row until Jacket measures 11 (13, 17, 21)" (28 [33, 43, 53]cm) from shoulder. End with a WS row.

Work 6 rows in garter st. BO all sts.

SLEEVES

Transfer 36 (43, 46, 50) held sts of Sleeve to DPN. Join yarn at back of Sleeve, pick up and knit 5 sts across underarm—42 (48, 52, 56) sts. (See page 155 in the Glossary for instructions on picking up sts.) Divide sts evenly over DPNs and place a marker for beg of rnd at center of underarm.

Knit 1 rnd.

DEC RND: K1, k2tog, knit to last 2 sts, ssk—40 (46, 50, 54) sts.

Cont in St st, rep Dec Rnd on every 2nd (2nd, 3rd, 4th) rnd 4 times more—32 (38, 42, 46) sts.

Work even until Sleeve measures 2 (2¾, 3¾, 4½)" (5 [7, 9, 11]cm) from underarm.

INC RND: K1, m1, knit to last st, m1, k1—34 (40, 44, 48) sts.

Rep Inc Rnd on every 3rd (3rd, 4th, 5th) rnd 5 (5, 4, 4) times more—44 (50, 52, 56) sts.

Work even until Sleeve measures 4¾ (5½, 7½, 8½)" (12 [14, 19, 22]cm) from underarm.

Work in garter st for 6 rnds. BO loosely in purl.

FINISHING

With DPN, CO 6 sts and work in I-cord for 33 (36, 39, 42)" (84 [91, 99, 107]cm). (See page 17 in the Learning the Basics section for step-by-step instructions on knitting I-cord.) Fasten off. Match center of cord to center back neck and stitch it in place all around the neckline, leaving about 8" (20cm) of cord free at each end for ties.

Weave in ends.

handy mittens

Make use of the rest of your Malabrigo skein (from the Swing Jacket, page 74) and knit up a quick pair of soft mittens. Don't skip the I-cord; it will prevent heartbreak by keeping mittens close at hand. Children's mittens are typically knitted with washable wool or acrylic, but pure wool mittens have a special feature. When your child plays in the snow, the mittens felt to fit the contours of her hand.

KNITTING SKILLS

I-cord: Knit a tube with 2 DPNs by knitting only 1 side of the work (see page 17)

k2tog [knit 2 together]: Dec by knitting 2 sts tog as 1 st (see page 14)

m1 [make 1]: Inc by picking up the bar between 2 sts from front to back, place it on the left-hand needle, then knit it through the back loop (see page 15)

St st [Stockinette stitch]: Knit on right side, purl on wrong side

Sizes
12 mos (2–4 yrs, 4–6 yrs)

Finished Measurements
Palm circumference: 4¾ (5½, 6)" (12 [14, 15]cm)

Yarn
partial skein Malabrigo Merino Worsted (merino wool, 215 yds [197m] per 100g skein), in color #157 Amoroso (leftovers from *Swing Jacket*, page 74, are sufficient)

Needles
2 size US 6 (4mm) circular needles
OR 1 set of 5 size US 6 (4mm) DPNs

Notions
scrap yarn
yarn needle

Gauge
20 sts and 28 rows = 4" (10cm) in St st

CUFF

CO 24 (28, 30) sts. Divide evenly over 2 circular needles (or DPNs) and join for working in the rnd, being careful not to twist sts. (See page 16 in the Learning the Basics section for step-by-step instructions on working in the rnd with 2 circular needles.) Work in k2, p2 rib for 2 (2¼, 2¾)" [5 (6, 7)cm]. Change to St st and work 3 rnds.

THUMB GUSSET

NEXT RND: K1, m1, knit to last st, m1, k1—26 (30, 32) sts.

Knit 2 rnds.

Rep last 3 rnds 1 (2, 2) times more—28 (34, 36) sts.

NEXT RND: Knit to last 3 (4, 4) sts, slip next 6 (8, 8) sts onto scrap yarn. (3 [4, 4] sts will come from one needle, and 3 [4, 4] sts will come from the other.) CO 2 sts over gap—24 (28, 30) sts. (See page 154 in the Glossary for instructions on casting on backward-loop style.)

HAND

Work even until Hand measures 3 (3½, 4¼)" [8 (9, 11)cm] from top of ribbing.

NEXT RND: *K2tog, k2; rep from * to end, end k2tog for largest size—18 (21, 22) sts.

Knit 1 rnd.

NEXT RND: *K2tog, k1; rep from * to end, end k1 for larger size—12 (14, 15) sts.

NEXT RND: K2tog around, end k1 for larger size—6 (7, 8) sts.

Break yarn, draw through rem sts and fasten off.

THUMB

Replace 6 (8, 8) sts from scrap yarn on needles. Pick up and knit 4 sts from Hand, where 2 sts were CO to bridge gap—10 (12, 12) sts. Join for working in the rnd.

Work even until Thumb measures ¾ (1, 1¼)" [2 (3, 3)cm] from picked-up sts.

NEXT RND: K2tog around—5 (6, 6) sts.

Break yarn, draw through rem sts and fasten off.

FINISHING

CO 3 sts and work in I-cord for 24 (30, 34)" (61 [76, 86]cm), or long enough to reach from one wrist behind the neck to the other. (See page 17 in the Learning the Basics section for step-by-step instructions on knitting I-cord.) Fasten off.

Attach ends of cord to Mitten Cuffs on side opposite Thumb.

Weave in ends.

CHUNKY PONCHO

Make this cozy cover-up for the perfect weekend project. Just grab three different colored skeins of soft yarn and size eleven circular needles, then settle yourself into a comfortable chair. Worked in the round from the bottom up, the poncho is a delight to knit. The combination of generous-sized needles, simple shaping and frequent color changes makes your progress quick and interesting. The only finishing is seaming the top of the pointed hood and making the playful pompom drawstring.

Sizes

24 mos (3–4 years, 5–6 years)

Finished Measurements

Hem edge circumference: 34 (38½, 44)" [86 (98, 112)cm]

Length from neck to point: 13 (15¾, 18¼)" [33 (40, 46)cm]

Yarn

1 (2, 3) skein(s) Debbie Bliss Cashmerino Superchunky (merino wool/microfiber/cashmere blend, 82 yds [75m] per 50g skein) in color #16002 lilac (A)

1 (2, 3) skein(s) Debbie Bliss Cashmerino Superchunky in color #16018 peas (B)

1 (2, 2) skein(s) Debbie Bliss Cashmerino Superchunky in color #16026 dark magenta (C)

Needles

24" (60cm) size US 11 (8mm) circular needle

Notions

crochet hook

stitch markers

yarn needle

Gauge

12 sts and 16 rows = 4" (10cm) in St st

KNITTING SKILLS

garter st [garter st]: Knit every row

k2tog [knit 2 together]: Dec by knitting 2 sts tog as 1 st (see page 14)

m1 [make 1]: Inc by picking up the bar between 2 sts from front to back, place it on the left-hand needle, then knit it through the back loop (see page 15)

p2tog [purl 2 together]: Dec by purling 2 sts tog as 1 st, just as for k2tog

pm [place marker]: Slide a marker onto the needle as indicated

sm [slip marker]: Slide a marker from 1 needle to the other as indicated

St st [Stockinette stitch]: Knit on right side, purl on wrong side; when working in the rnd, knit every row

BODY

With yarn A, CO 104 (116, 132) sts. Join for working in the rnd, being careful not to twist sts.

RND 1: K26 (29, 33), pm for center front, k26 (29, 33), pm for side "seam," k26 (29, 33), pm for center back, k26 (29, 33), pm for second side seam/beg of rnd.

Purl 1 rnd, knit 1 rnd, purl 1 rnd. Change to St st and work 3 (5, 7) rnds.

DEC RND: Knit to 2 sts before center front marker, k2tog, sm, k2tog. Knit to 2 sts before center back marker, k2tog, sm, k2tog—100 (112, 128) sts.

Knit 3 (5, 7) rnds. Rep Dec Rnd—96 (108, 124) sts.

Knit 3 (5, 7) rnds. Change to yarn C. Rep Dec Rnd—92 (104, 120) sts.

Knit 2 (3, 3) rnds. Change to yarn B. Rep Dec Rnd—88 (100, 116) sts.

Knit 2 (4, 4) rnds. Rep Dec Rnd—84 (96, 112) sts.

Knit 2 (3, 4) rnds. Rep Dec Rnd—80 (92, 108) sts.

Knit 2 (3, 4) rnds. Change to yarn A.

NEXT RND: Purl to 2 sts before center front marker, p2tog, sm, p2tog. Purl to 2 sts before center back marker, p2tog, sm, p2tog—76 (88, 104) sts.

Purl 1 rnd. Change to yarn C. Knit 1 rnd. Rep Dec Rnd—72 (84, 100) sts.

Knit 7 rnds.

FRONT NECK OPENING

NEXT RND: Knit to center front marker. K3, k2tog, knit to 2 sts before side seam marker, k2tog, sm, k2tog. Knit to 2 sts before center back marker, k2tog, sm, k2tog. Knit to 2 sts before side seam marker, k2tog, sm, k2tog. Knit to 5 sts before center front marker, k2tog, k3—64 (76, 92) sts. Turn.

Note: Neck Opening and Hood are worked back and forth in rows from this point on.

NEXT ROW: K3, purl to last 3 sts, k3.

Keeping first and last 3 sts of each row in garter st, work 2 rows even. Change to yarn B.

NEXT ROW (RS): K3, k2tog, knit to 2 sts before side seam marker, k2tog, sm, k2tog. Knit to 2 sts before center back marker, k2tog, sm, k2tog. Knit to 2 sts before side seam marker, k2tog, sm, k2tog. Knit to last 5 sts, k2tog, k3—56 (68, 84) sts.

Work 1 row even. Rep last RS row—48 (60, 76) sts.

SIZE 5–6 YEARS ONLY: Work 1 row even. Rep last RS row—68 sts.

ALL SIZES: Change to yarn A. Purl 2 rows.

Change to yarn C. Purl 1 row.

NEXT ROW (RS): P3, k2tog, knit to 2 sts before side seam marker, k2tog, sm, k2tog. Knit to 2 sts before center back marker, k2tog, sm, k2tog. Knit to 2 sts before side seam marker, k2tog, sm, k2tog. Knit to last 5 sts, k2tog, k3—40 (52, 60) sts.

Work 1 row even.

NEXT ROW (RS): P6, k2tog, knit to last 8 sts, k2tog, p6—38 (50, 58) sts.

NEXT ROW (WS): BO 6 sts, purl to last 6 sts, BO 6—26 (38, 46) sts.

Remove any rem markers.

HOOD

Change to yarn B.

ROW 1 (RS): K13 (19, 23), pm, k13 (19, 23).

ROW 2 AND ALL EVEN ROWS (WS): K3, purl to last 3 sts, k3.

ROW 3: Knit to 1 st before m, m1, k1, sm, k1, m1, knit to end—28 (40, 48) sts.

ROW 5: K3, m1, knit to 1 st before m, m1, k1, sm, k1, m1, knit to last 3 sts, yo, knit to end—32 (44, 52) sts.

ROW 7: Rep Row 3—34 (46, 54) sts.

ROW 9: Rep Row 5—38 (50, 58) sts.

ROW 11: Rep Row 3—40 (52, 60) sts.

Work 1 (3, 5) rows even.

Change to yarn A. Knit 2 rows. Purl 1 row.

Change to yarn C. Work 4 (6, 6) rows even in St st, keeping 3 sts at each edge in garter st.

Change to yarn B.

Work 1 row even.

NEXT ROW (RS): Knit to 1 st before m, m1, k1, sm, k1, m1, knit to end—42 (54, 62) sts.

Rep last 2 rows 4 (5, 6) times more—50 (64, 74) sts.

Work 4 rows even. BO all sts.

FINISHING
Fold Hood in half, with right sides facing, and sew top seam.

Ties: Crochet a 16" (41cm) chain with yarn B for front tie. Lace it through the knitting crisscross fashion, on either side of front opening. (See page 21 in Learning the Basics for step-by-step instructions on crocheting a chain.)

Pompoms (make 2): Wrap yarn A around your fingers to make a 2" (5cm) pompom. Secure the center of the pompom with scrap yarn. Thread yarn tail at either end of chain onto a tapestry needle and stitch it to the pompoms.

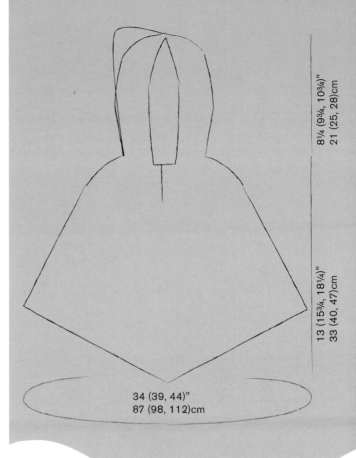

8¼ (9¾, 10¾)"
21 (25, 28)cm

13 (15¾, 18¼)"
33 (40, 47)cm

34 (39, 44)"
87 (98, 112)cm

fuzzy Bolero sweater

Pattern by Chesley Flotten

WRAP THIS LUXURIOUS SWEATER AROUND YOUR PRECIOUS LITTLE PRINCESS TO KEEP WINTER'S CHILL AT BAY. The short bolero length is the ideal cover-up for dresses—it keeps chest and arms warm while leaving legs free. Cleverly designed by Chesley Flotten, it's knit in one piece from the top down, with no seams. True to its name, Softy yarn is lovely to touch and features fluffy little bumps that add texture to your knitting.

KNITTING SKILLS

kfb [knit 1 front and back]: Inc by knitting into the front and back of the next st (see page 15)

k2tog [knit 2 together]: Dec by knitting 2 sts tog as 1 st (see page 14)

m1 [make 1]: Inc by picking up the bar between 2 sts from front to back, place it on the left-hand needle, then knit it through the back loop (see page 15)

pm [place marker]: Slide a marker onto the needle as indicated

sm [slip marker]: Slide a marker from one needle to the other as indicated

ssk [slip, slip, knit]: Sl the first st as if to knit, slip the second st as if to knit, then bring the left needle through both sts from front to back and knit them tog to create a left-leaning dec

Sizes
9–12 (18–24) mos

Finished Measurements
Chest: 23 (25)" [58 (64)cm]
Length from shoulder: 6¼ (7)" [16 (18)cm]

Yarn
3 (4) skeins Berroco Softy (DuPont Tactel® nylon/nylon blend, 104 yds [96m] per 50g skein) in color #2901 Snow Bunny

Needles
24" (60cm) size US 8 (5mm) circular needles
1 set of 5 size US 8 (5mm) DPNs

Notions
scrap yarn
stitch markers
yarn needle
⅔ yd (⅝m) 1" (3cm) wide satin ribbon

Gauge
20 sts and 28 rows = 4" (10cm) in St st

Note: The Bolero is knit in one piece from the neck down.

YOKE

With circular needle, CO 2 sts, pm, CO 14 sts, pm, CO 19 (21) sts, pm, CO 14 sts, pm, CO 2 sts—51 (53) sts.

ROW 1 (RS): Kfb twice, sm, kfb, *knit to 1 st before next marker, kfb, sm, kfb; rep from * to last st, kfb—61 (63) sts.

Note: Do not join for working in the rnd.

ROW 2 (WS): Purl.

ROW 3: K1, m1, *knit to 1 st before marker, kfb, sm, kfb; rep from * 3 times, knit to last st, m1, k1—71 (73) sts.

ROW 4: Purl.

Rep Rows 3–4, 7 (7) times more until 37 (39) sts rem between markers—141 (143) sts.

NEXT ROW (RS): *Knit to 1 st before marker, kfb, sm, kfb; rep from * 3 times, knit to end—149 (151) sts.

NEXT ROW: Purl.

Rep last 2 rows until 55 sts rem between back markers—213 (215) sts.

NEXT ROW (RS): Removing markers as you go, ssk, knit to first marker, slip all sts between first and second markers to a piece of scrap yarn (these sts will become a Sleeve). CO 3 (4) sts to the tip of the right needle. Knit to third marker, slip all sts between third and fourth markers to a piece of scrap yarn (sts for second Sleeve). CO 3 (4) sts backward-loop style to the tip of the right needle. (See page 154 in the Glossary for instructions on casting on backward-loop style.) Knit to last 2 sts, k2tog.

There are 119 (123) sts on needle.

BODY

NEXT ROW (WS): Purl.

DEC ROW (RS): Ssk, knit to last 2 sts, k2tog—117 (121) sts.

Rep last 2 rows 1 (3) times more—115 (119) sts.

NEXT ROW (WS): Knit.

Rep Dec Row.

Rep last 2 rows once more—111 (115) sts.

NEXT ROW (WS): Knit.

BO loosely.

SLEEVES (MAKE 2)

Transfer the sts of one Sleeve from scrap yarn to 2 circular needles or to DPNs—49 (49) sts. Join yarn at back of arm. Pick up and knit 7 sts from underarm—56 (56) sts. (See page 155 in the Glossary for instructions on picking up sts.) Divide sts evenly over 2 circular needles or over DPNs, place marker for beg of rnd at center of underarm, and join for working in the rnd. (See page 16 in the Learning the Basics section for step-by-step instructions on working in the rnd with 2 circular needles.) Knit 1 rnd.

DEC RND: K1, k2tog, knit to last 2 sts, ssk—54 (54).

Knit 3 rnds.

Rep last 4 rnds until 38 (40) sts rem.

Work even until Sleeve measures 5 (5¾)" [13 (15)cm] from underarm.

Purl 1 rnd, knit 1 rnd, then purl 1 more rnd. BO loosely.

FINISHING

FRONT AND NECK EDGING

Beg at bottom right front, with RS facing and circular needle, pick up and knit 30 (34) sts along front edge, 12 sts across shoulder, 16 (18) sts across back neck, 12 sts across shoulder, and 30 (34) sts down left front—100 (110) sts. Work 3 rows in garter st. BO loosely.

Weave in ends. Draw ribbon through front neck edges and tie.

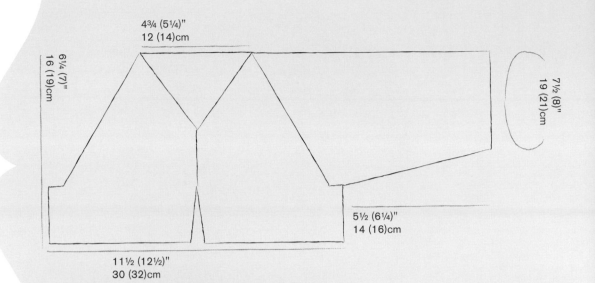

4¾ (5¼)"
12 (14)cm

6¼ (7)"
16 (19)cm

7½ (8)"
19 (21)cm

5½ (6¼)"
14 (16)cm

11½ (12½)"
30 (32)cm

 SHAGGY VEST

I COULDN'T PASS UP THE SOFTY YARN, AND I WANTED TO KNIT UP THIS FUNKY SHAGGY VEST FOR CELIA MYSELF. It will most likely be worn for fun, but its inherent warmth does make it practical, too. Paired with jeans and a long-sleeved shirt, the vest makes a comfortable fall or winter outfit. I love the dimension of the yarn, and how the color varies with the bumps. You could almost get away without finishing the edges.

KNITTING SKILLS

garter st [garter st]: Knit every row

k2tog [knit 2 together]: Dec by knitting 2 sts tog as 1 st (see page 14)

kfb [knit 1 front and back]: Inc by knitting 1 in the front and back of the next st (see page 15)

St st [Stockinette stitch]: Knit on right side, purl on wrong side

Sizes
3–4 (4–5, 5–6) years

Finished Measurements
Chest: 26 (28, 30, 32)" [66 (71, 76, 81)cm]
Length: 11 (12, 13, 14)" [28 (30, 33, 36)cm]

Yarn
3 (3, 3, 4) skeins Berroco Softy (DuPont Tactel® nylon/nylon blend, 104 yds [96m] per 50g skein) in color #2941 Bella Donna

Needles
size US 8 (5mm) straight needles

Notions
crochet hook
yarn needle

Gauge
20 sts and 28 rows = 4" (10cm) in St st

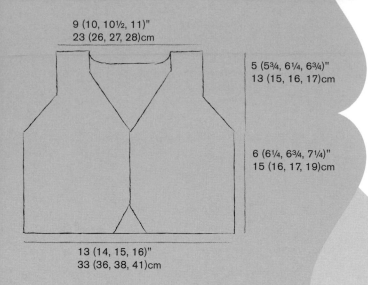

9 (10, 10½, 11)"
23 (26, 27, 28)cm

5 (5¾, 6¼, 6¾)"
13 (15, 16, 17)cm

6 (6¼, 6¾, 7¼)"
15 (16, 17, 19)cm

13 (14, 15, 16)"
33 (36, 38, 41)cm

BACK

CO 52 (56, 60, 64) sts. Work 6 rows in garter st. Cont in St st until piece measures 6 (6¼, 6¾, 7¼)" [15 (16, 17, 18)cm] from cast-on edge, ending with a WS row.

ARMHOLE SHAPING

NEXT ROW (RS): K2tog, knit to last 2 sts, k2tog—50 (54, 58, 62) sts.

NEXT ROW: Purl.

Rep last 2 rows 7 (7, 8, 9) times more—36 (40, 42, 44) sts.

Work even until Armhole measures 4¼ (5, 5½, 6)" [11 (13, 14, 15)cm], ending with a WS row.

SHOULDER AND NECK SHAPING

NEXT ROW (RS): K10 (11, 12, 12), BO 16 (18, 18, 20), knit to end.

LEFT SHOULDER

NEXT ROW: Purl.

NEXT ROW: K2tog, knit to end—9 (10, 11, 11) sts.

Rep last 2 rows once more—8 (9, 10, 10) sts.

BO.

RIGHT SHOULDER

Rejoin yarn at neck edge and purl 1 WS row.

NEXT ROW: Knit to last 2 sts, k2tog—9 (10, 11, 11) sts.

Rep last 2 rows once more—8 (9, 10, 10) sts.

BO.

LEFT FRONT

CO 22 (24, 26, 28) sts. Work 6 rows in garter st.

INC ROW (RS): Knit to last st, kfb—23 (25, 27, 29) sts.

NEXT ROW: Purl.

Rep last 2 rows 3 times more—26 (28, 30, 32) sts.

Cont in St st until piece measures 6 (6¼, 6¾, 7¼)" [15 (16, 17, 18)cm] from cast-on edge, ending with a WS row.

NECK AND ARMHOLE SHAPING

NEXT ROW (RS): K2tog, knit to last 2 sts, k2tog—24 (26, 28, 30) sts.

NEXT ROW: Purl.

Rep last 2 rows 7 (7, 8, 9) times more—10 (12, 12, 12) sts.

NEXT ROW (RS): Knit to last 2 sts, k2tog—9 (11, 11, 11) sts.

NEXT ROW: Purl.

Rep last 2 rows 1 (2, 1, 1) time(s) more—8 (9, 10, 10) sts.

Work even until Armhole measures same as Back to Shoulder. BO.

RIGHT FRONT

CO 22 (24, 26, 28) sts. Work 6 rows in garter st.

INC ROW (RS): Kfb, knit to end—23 (25, 27, 29) sts.

NEXT ROW: Purl.

Rep last 2 rows 3 times more—26 (28, 30, 32) sts.

Cont in St st until piece measures 6 (6¼, 6¾, 7¼)" [15 (16, 17, 18)cm] from cast-on edge, ending with a WS row.

TIP

To make the knitting go more quickly, work both of the fronts at the same time on a single pair of needles. Cast on with a separate ball of yarn for each front. Then just reverse the shaping for one front piece.

NECK AND ARMHOLE SHAPING

NEXT ROW (RS): K2tog, knit to last 2 sts, k2tog—24 (26, 28, 30) sts.

NEXT ROW: Purl.

Rep last 2 rows 7 (7, 8, 9) times more—10 (12, 12, 12) sts.

NEXT ROW (RS): K2tog, knit to end—9 (11, 11, 11) sts.

NEXT ROW: Purl.

Rep last 2 rows 1 (2, 1, 1) time(s) more—8 (9, 10, 10) sts.

Work even until Armhole measures same as Back to Shoulder. BO.

FINISHING

Seam shoulders. Sew side seams, leaving bottom 1½" (4cm) open.

Optional: This vest has a loose, unstructured quality, but I chose to finish the exposed edges with a row of single crochet around the front and neck edges and each armhole. This finish doesn't add width to any of the dimensions, but it does help to stabilize the edges.

Front tie: Crochet a chain 14" (36cm) long. Draw each end through one side of the front and tie it in a loose knot. (See page 21 in the Learning the Basics section for step-by-step instructions on crocheting a chain.)

shark pullover

DON'T WORRY THAT LITTLE FINGERS MIGHT BE NIBBLED IN THE SHARK POCKET PULLOVER. Fleece yarn is as soft as can be—this is a sweater children want to wear for comfort and for fun. They'll spin in circles trying to see the little shark on the back swimming away from the big shark on the front. If you haven't worked with fleece before, I'm sure you'll love how quickly it knits together and instantly camouflages any irregularities in your stitches. Lightweight yet warm, I'm keeping one in our beach bag for when the sea breeze picks up in the afternoons.

Sizes
12 mos (24 mos, 4 yrs, 6 yrs)

Finished Measurements
Chest: 23 (26, 28, 30)" [58 (66, 71, 76)cm]
Length: 10 (11, 12, 14)" [25 (28, 30, 36)cm]

Yarn
3 (3, 3, 4) skeins Knit One Crochet Too Fleece (polyester, 109 yds [100m] per 50g) in color #784 Grape (MC)
1 skein each Knit One Crochet Too Fleece in color #353 Coral (CC1) and in color #531 Lime (CC2)

Needles
size US 9 (5.5mm) straight needles

Notions
2 ¾" (19mm) buttons
2 small "anchor" buttons
stitch holder
stitch markers
yarn needle

Gauge
12 sts and 16 rows = 4" (10cm) in St st

KNITTING SKILLS

garter st [garter st]: Knit every row

Intarsia: Work in a two-color pattern by picking up a new color and twisting it around the other color at the back of the work (see page 18)

k2tog [knit 2 together]: Dec by knitting 2 sts tog as 1 st (see page 14)

m1 [make 1]: Inc by picking up the bar between 2 sts from front to back, place it on the left-hand needle, then knit it through the back loop (see page 15)

pm [place marker]: Slide a marker onto the needle as indicated

St st [Stockinette stitch]: Knit on right side, purl on wrong side

yo [yarn over]: Wrap the yarn once around the right-hand needle and cont knitting; on subsequent row, treat the wrap as a st, creating an eyelet hole in the knitted fabric

Note: When working chart patterns, twist yarns at color changes to prevent gaps. (See page 18 in the Learning the Basics section for step-by-step instructions on this technique.)

BACK

With MC, CO 34 (39, 42, 45) sts. Work 4 rows in garter st. Change to St st and work 6 (8, 10, 12) rows, beg with a RS row.

NEXT ROW (RS): K14 (17, 19, 21), pm, work Row 1 of Small Shark Chart over next 15 sts, pm, knit to end.

Cont as est, working Small Shark Chart between markers, through all 12 rows of chart.

Work even, if necessary, until piece measures 5¼ (6, 6½, 7½)" [13 (15, 17, 19)cm] from cast-on edge, ending with a WS row.

ARMHOLE SHAPING

NEXT ROW (RS): K2tog, knit to last 2 sts, k2tog—32 (37, 40, 43) sts.

NEXT ROW: Purl.

Rep last 2 rows twice more—28 (33, 36, 39) sts.

Work even until Armhole measures 4¾ (5, 5½, 6)" [12 (13, 14, 15)cm], ending with a WS row.

SHOULDER AND NECK SHAPING

BO 6 (8, 8, 9) sts at beg of next 2 rows—16 (17, 20, 21) sts.

Work 3 rows garter st. BO all sts.

FRONT

Work as for Back until Armhole measures 1¾ (2, 2, 2½)" [5 (5, 5, 6½)cm], ending with a WS row.

RIGHT NECK PLACKET

NEXT ROW: K12 (15, 16, 18) and place these sts on a holder. Knit rem 16 (18, 20, 21) sts.

NEXT ROW: Purl to last 4 sts, k4.

NEXT ROW: Knit.

Work as est, keeping 4 placket sts in garter st, for ¾ (¾, 1¼, 1¼)" [2 (2, 3, 3)cm], ending with a WS row.

BUTTONHOLE ROW: K1, yo, k2tog, knit to end.

Work even for 1 (1, 1½, 1½)" [3 (3, 4, 4)cm].

NEXT ROW: Rep Buttonhole Row.

Work even until Armhole measures same as Back to Shoulder, ending with a RS row.

RIGHT SHOULDER

NEXT ROW (WS): BO 6 (8, 8, 9) sts, knit to end.

Knit 2 rows. BO.

LEFT NECK PLACKET

Replace held sts on needle with WS facing. Use backward-loop method to CO 4 sts on right-hand needle with CC2, then p16 (18, 20, 21) with MC—20 (22, 24, 25) sts. (See page 154 in the Glossary for instructions on casting on backward-loop style.)

NEXT ROW (RS): Knit to last 4 sts with MC, k4 with CC2. Twist yarns at color change to prevent gaps.

NEXT ROW: K4 with CC2, purl to end with MC.

Work as est, keeping 4 placket sts in garter st in CC2, until Armhole measures same as Back to Shoulder, ending with a WS row.

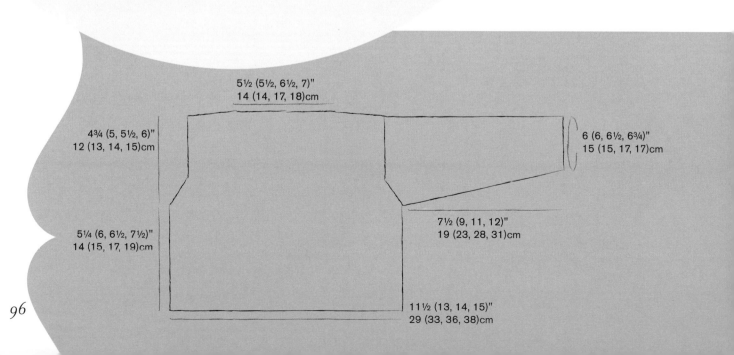

5½ (5½, 6½, 7)"
14 (14, 17, 18)cm

4¾ (5, 5½, 6)"
12 (13, 14, 15)cm

6 (6, 6½, 6¾)"
15 (15, 17, 17)cm

5¼ (6, 6½, 7½)"
14 (15, 17, 19)cm

7½ (9, 11, 12)"
19 (23, 28, 31)cm

11½ (13, 14, 15)"
29 (33, 36, 38)cm

LEFT SHOULDER

NEXT ROW (RS): BO 6 (8, 8, 9) sts, purl to end.

Purl 2 rows. BO all sts.

SLEEVES (MAKE 2)

With MC, CO 18 (18, 19, 20) sts. Work 4 rows in garter st.

Inc 1 st at each end of next row—20 (20, 21, 22) sts.

Cont in St st, inc 1 st at each end of every 5th row 4 (5, 6, 7) times—28 (30, 33, 36) sts.

Work even until Sleeve measures 7½ (9, 11, 12)" [19 (23, 28, 31)cm] from cast-on edge. BO all sts.

POCKET

With MC, CO 21 (24, 24, 28) sts.

FOR 12 MOS SIZE:

Beg with a purl row, work 3 rows in St st.

NEXT ROW (RS): K3, work Row 1 of Small Shark Chart over next 15 sts, k3.

NEXT ROW (WS): P3, work Row 2 of Small Shark Chart over next 15 sts, p3.

Rep last 2 rows 4 times more, for a total of 12 rows from cast-on edge.

NEXT ROW (RS): K2tog, k1, work Chart patt as est over 15 sts, k1, k2tog—19 sts.

NEXT ROW (WS): P2, work Chart patt as est over 15 sts, p2.

Chart patt is now complete.

NEXT ROW (RS): K2tog, knit to last 2 sts, k2tog—17 sts.

NEXT ROW (WS): Purl.

Rep last 2 rows once more—15 sts.

BO.

FOR ALL OTHER SIZES:

Work in St st following Large Shark Chart. If making size 6 sweater, you will have 2 extra sts on either side of Chart patt. Work these in St st.

On Row 18, Chart begins to narrow. K2tog at beg and end of each row to match Chart shaping.

When Chart patt is complete, BO.

FINISHING

Join Shoulder seams. Sew Sleeves into Armholes. Sew top and bottom of Pocket to Front of sweater, centering Pocket about 1¼" (3cm) above cast-on edge. Sew side and Sleeve seams. Tack bottom of Left Neck Placket behind Right Placket. Attach buttons to Left Placket, anchoring them with smaller buttons on WS of work. Weave in ends.

SMALL SHARK CHART

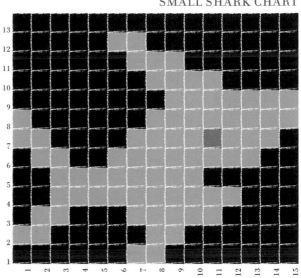

LARGE SHARK CHART   Blank squares indicate Pocket shaping.

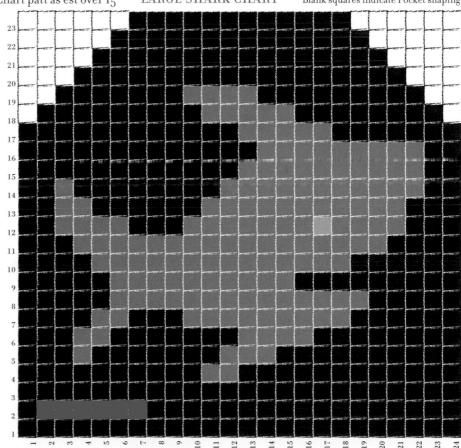

STRIPED VESTS

THIS VEST WILL KEEP YOUR BUSY TODDLER WARM WHILE LEAVING ACTIVE ARMS FREE FOR GETTING MESSY AND EXPLORING. Perfect for beginners, this vest is knit in the round all the way up to the armholes where it splits in two so the front and back can be worked separately. You end up with a single piece of knitting—no sewing required. Just weave in the ends and add buttons. Superwash yarn launders easily in the washing machine, making this vest a practical way to add color to everyday wear.

KNITTING SKILLS

garter st [garter stitch]: Knit every row

k2tog [knit 2 together]: Dec by knitting 2 sts tog as 1 st (see page 14)

pm [place marker]: Slide a marker onto the needle as indicated

sm [slip marker]: Slide a marker from one needle to the other as indicated

St st [Stockinette stitch]: Knit on right side, purl on wrong side; when working in the rnd, knit every row

yo [yarn over]: Wrap the yarn once around the right-hand needle and cont knitting; on the subsequent row, treat the wrap as a st, creating an eyelet hole in the knitted fabric

Sizes
9–12 mos (18–24 mos, 3–4 yrs, 5–6 yrs)

Finished Measurements
Chest: 20 (23, 25, 27)" [51 (58, 64, 69)cm]
Length: 10½ (11¾, 12¼, 13¼)" [27 (30, 31, 34)cm]

Yarn
1 (1, 2, 2) skein(s) Cascade Yarns 220 Superwash (superwash wool, 220 yds [201m] per 100g skein) in color # 808 red (MC) or color #802 green (MC1)

1 skein Cascade 220 in color #829 pink (CC) or color #819 brown (CC1)

Needles
16" (40cm) size US 7 (4.5mm) circular needle

Notions
2 1" (25mm) buttons
stitch holder
stitch markers
yarn needle

Gauge
18 sts and 24 rows = 4" (10cm) in St st

LOWER BODY

With CC, CO 90 (104, 112, 122) sts. Join for working in the rnd and pm.

Work 16 rnds in garter st.

Change to MC and cont in St st until piece measures 5½ (6, 6, 6½)" [14 (15, 15, 17)cm] from cast-on edge. Stop knitting last rnd 3 (4, 4, 5) sts before marker.

ARMHOLES

NEXT RND: BO 6 (8, 8, 10) sts, knit until there are 39 (44, 48, 51) sts on right-hand needle, BO 6 (8, 8, 10) sts, knit to end.

Place 39 (44, 48, 51) sts for Front of Vest on a holder.

UPPER BACK

Working on 39 (44, 48, 51) sts still on needle, purl 1 WS row.

NEXT ROW (RS): K2tog, knit to last 2 sts, k2tog—37 (42, 46, 49) sts.

NEXT ROW: Purl.

Rep last 2 rows 0 (1, 2, 2) times more—37 (40, 42, 45) sts.

Work even until Armhole measures 1¼ (1¾, 2¼, 2¾)" [3 (4, 6, 7)cm], ending with a WS row.

NECK AND SHOULDER STRAPS

Change to CC and work 12 rows in garter st.

Change to MC and knit 1 row.

NEXT ROW (WS): K13 (14, 14, 15), BO 11 (12, 14, 15) sts, knit to end.

RIGHT STRAP

As you knit Straps, change colors every 2 rows. Do not cut color not in use, but carry it up the side of the work.

NEXT ROW (RS): Knit to last 2 sts, k2tog—12 (13, 13, 14) sts.

Knit 1 row.

NEXT ROW: Knit to last 2 sts, k2tog—11 (12, 12, 13) sts.

**Work even in garter st, remembering to change colors, until Armhole measures 6½ (7, 7½, 8¼)" [17 (18, 19, 21)cm].

K2tog at beg of next 2 rows—9 (10, 10, 11) sts.

BUTTONHOLE ROW: K4 (4, 4, 5), yo, k2tog, k3 (4, 4, 4).

Knit 2 rows.

NEXT ROW: K2tog, knit to last 2 sts, k2tog—7 (8, 8, 9) sts.

Knit 1 row.

NEXT ROW: K2tog, knit to last 2 sts, k2tog-—5 (6, 6, 7) sts.

BO all sts.

LEFT STRAP

Rejoin yarn at neck edge with RS facing and knit 1 row.

NEXT ROW (WS): Knit to last 2 sts, k2tog—12 (13, 13, 14) sts.

Knit 1 row.

NEXT ROW: Knit to last 2 sts, k2tog—11 (12, 12, 13) sts.

Cont as for Right Strap from **.

UPPER FRONT

Replace 39 (44, 48, 51) sts from holder on needle. Rejoin MC at Armhole edge with WS facing and purl 1 row.

NEXT ROW (RS): K2tog, knit to last 2 sts, k2tog—37 (42, 46, 49) sts.

NEXT ROW: Purl.

Rep last 2 rows 0 (1, 2, 2) times more—37 (40, 42, 45) sts.

Work even until Armhole measures 1¼ (1¾, 2¼, 2¾)" [3 (4, 6, 7)cm], ending with a WS row.

Work 8 rows in garter st.

Change to CC and knit 1 row.

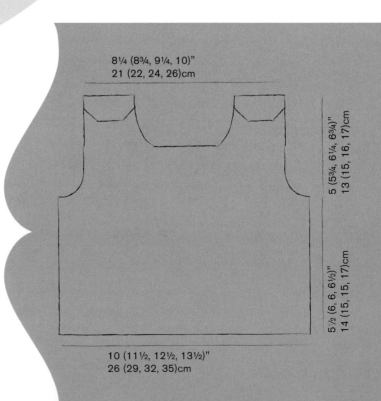

8¼ (8¾, 9¼, 10)"
21 (22, 24, 26)cm

5 (5¾, 6¼, 6¾)"
13 (15, 16, 17)cm

5½ (6, 6, 6½)"
14 (15, 15, 17)cm

10 (11½, 12½, 13½)"
26 (29, 32, 35)cm

NECK AND SHOULDER STRAPS

NEXT ROW (WS): K13 (14, 14, 15), BO 11 (12, 14, 15) sts, knit to end.

RIGHT STRAP

As you work Straps, change colors every 2 rows as for Back.

NEXT ROW (RS): Knit to last 2 sts, k2tog—12 (13, 13, 14) sts.

NEXT ROW: Knit.

Rep last 2 rows 3 times more—9 (10, 10, 11) sts.

Work even in garter st until Armhole measures 4 (4½, 5¼, 5¾)" [10 (11, 13, 15)cm. BO all sts.

LEFT STRAP

Rejoin yarn at neck edge with RS facing and knit 1 row.

NEXT ROW (WS): Knit to last 2 sts, k2tog—12 (13, 13, 14) sts.

NEXT ROW: Knit.

Rep last 2 rows 3 times more—9 (10, 10, 11) sts.

Work even in garter st until Armhole measures 4 (4½, 5¼, 5¾)" [10 (11, 13, 15)cm. BO all sts.

FINISHING

Weave in ends. Attach buttons.

castle purse + finger puppets

When I first finished this toy, I brought it to the Knitting Experience Café to see what the reaction would be. Chesley's son took an immediate interest in the setup and instantly brought the finger puppet characters to life. He created an elaborate story that involved the knight, king and dragon all taking flight. When the front handle of the Castle Purse is lowered, the drawbridge opens to reveal the window and door openings, perfectly sized for the puppets to fit through. When the adventure is over, simply drop the puppets inside and pull the handle up to close the castle for transport. The cast of castle characters are quickly knit up in the round. Feel free to experiment—if you know your child is crazy about horses, don't stop at one…you can easily make more in different colors. If it's not a surprise gift, let them be part of the decision process so their imaginations can start setting the scene before they have the finished toy in their hands.

KNITTING SKILLS

garter st [garter st]: Knit every row

k2tog [knit 2 together]: Dec by knitting 2 sts tog as 1 st (see page 14)

m1 [make 1]: Inc by picking up the bar between 2 sts from front to back, place it on the left-hand needle, then knit it through the back loop (see page 15)

St st [Stockinette stitch]: Knit on right side, purl on wrong side

Notions
crochet hook
4 craft sticks
scrap yarn
stitch holders
yarn needle

Gauge
18 sts and 24 rows = 4" (10cm) in St st

Finished Measurements
approx 7½" x 5" x 2" (19cm x 13cm x 5cm)

Yarn
1 skein Cascade Yarns 220 Quatro (wool, 220 yds [201m] per 100g skein) in color #9437 variegated blue (MC)

small amounts of worsted weight wool in red, pink, green, brown, orange, and yellow

Needles
size US 7 (4.5mm) straight needles

2 size US 7 (4.5mm) circular needles

OR 1 set of 5 size US 7 (4.5mm) DPNs

CASTLE

With straight needles and MC, CO 30 sts.

Work in garter st for 8" (20cm). This is the back and base of the bag.

NEXT ROW (FRONT OPENING): K12, join second strand of yarn, BO 6, k12.

Work each side separately in garter st for 9 rows.

NEXT ROW: K12, CO 6, k12. Break extra yarn.

Work 4 rows in garter st.

NEXT ROW (WINDOW OPENINGS): K9, join second strand of yarn, BO 4, k4, join third strand of yarn, BO 4, k9.

Work all 3 sections separately for 6 rows.

NEXT ROW: K9, CO 4, k4, CO 4, k9. Break extra yarns.

Work 6 rows even.

RAMPARTS

NEXT ROW: K6 and place on holder, BO 6, k6 and place on holder, BO 6, k6.

Knit 4 rows on rem 6 sts on needle. BO.

One at a time, slip each section of 6 held sts back to needle, join yarn, knit 4 rows, and BO.

From cast-on edge of bag and with RS facing, pick up and knit 6 sts. (See page 155 in the Glossary for instructions on picking up sts.) Knit 4 rows, BO. Rep twice more, spacing Ramparts to match other end of bag.

SIDES (MAKE 2)

Fold the finished piece in half crosswise and mark the center on either side by tying on a contrasting bit of scrap yarn. Working on one side at a time, CO 3 sts, with RS facing pick up and knit 5 sts on either side of marker, CO 3 sts—16 sts.

There should be approx 4½" (11cm) of Castle front and back on either side of your picked-up sts.

ROW 1 (WS): K3, p10, k3.

ROW 2 (RS): Knit.

Rep Rows 1—2 until side measures 4½" (11cm).

BO 5 sts at beg of next 2 rows—6 sts.

Work 4 rows in garter st. BO.

To sew the side, first fold it up and position it between the front and back of the Castle. The garter st edging should lie underneath the front and back pieces, creating corner pockets for the craft sticks. With MC, stitch up both sides of each garter st panel to connect the corners. Slide the craft sticks into the narrow pocket and stitch the top closed.

TRIM

With yellow yarn and DPNs, pick up and knit 18 sts around each window opening. BO. With green yarn, pick up and knit 26 sts around the door opening. BO.

DRAWBRIDGE

Working 4 rows beneath the door opening, with RS facing and red yarn, pick up and knit 16 sts for the drawbridge (beg and ending 5 sts to either side of door opening).

ROW 1 (WS): Knit.

ROW 2 (RS): K3, p10, k3. (Note: the RS is the one that will show when the drawbridge is up.)

Rep these 2 rows for 3½" (9cm).

Work 6 rows in garter st. BO.

PENNANTS (MAKE 2)

With orange yarn, working on RS 1 row above the windows and 2 sts outside of them, pick up and knit 6 sts.

Work 4 rows in garter st, then 3 rows in St st. Cont in St st, k2tog at beg of next 2 rows—4 sts.

Work 4 rows garter st. Change to St st, k2tog at beg of next row—3 sts.

Work 2 rows St st. Cont in St st, k2tog at beg of next row—2 sts.

K2tog and fasten off.

Use yarn tail to tack the end of the Pennant to the Castle. With green yarn, embroider a five-pointed star on the Pennant.

HANDLES

Cut 2 16" (41cm) strands each of blue, green and red yarn. Make a double knot to join the strands together 1" (3cm) from the ends. Pair the colors together and tightly braid the whole length of the strands.

Thread all 6 strands through the eye of a large tapestry needle. Close the drawbridge up against the front of the castle. Bring the needle down through the top of the Drawbridge and then through the top of the Castle, between the Pennant and window. Bring the needle back out between the other window and Pennant and then stitch it through the other side of the Drawbridge. Test the Drawbridge, making sure it can open freely and lie flat on a tabletop without distorting the top of the Castle. Once you've made any necessary adjustments, tie a double knot and trim the ends, leaving 1" (3cm) of yarn to extend beyond the knot. Rep the process to make a Handle on the back of the Castle. Using the front Handle as your guide to position the back Handle, make sure the decorative knots lie on the outside. Match the length of the back Handle to the front Handle in the carrying position.

PUPPETS

DRAGON PUPPET WITH HORSE VARIATION

With 2 circular needles, or with DPNs, and green (orange) yarn, CO 8 sts. Join for working in the rnd, taking care not to twist sts. (See page 16 in the Learning the Basics section for step-by-step instructions on working in the rnd with 2 circular needles.) Work 7 rnds in St st.

NEXT RND: K1, m1, k6, m1, k1—10 sts.

Knit 1 rnd.

NEXT RND: K1, m1, k8, m1, k1—12 sts.

Knit 1 rnd.

NEXT RND: K1, m1, k2, k2tog, k2, k2tog, k2, m1, k1—12 sts.

Knit 1 rnd.

NEXT RND: K1, k2, k2tog, k2, k2tog, k2, k1—10 sts.

NEXT RND: K2, k2tog, k2, k2tog, k2—8 sts.

NEXT RND: K1, k2tog, k2, k2tog, k1—6 sts.

NEXT RND: K1, k2tog twice, k1—4 sts.

NEXT RND: K2tog twice—2 sts.

K2tog and fasten off.

TO FINISH THE DRAGON

Turn the knitting inside out so the reverse St st is on the outside (looks like dragon scales).

With yellow yarn, crochet a chain 8" (20cm) long. (See page 21 in the Learning the Basics section for step-by-step instructions on crocheting a chain.) Thread the yarn tail through a needle and tack it to the Dragon's back in loops: shorter ½" (1cm) loops at the head and larger 1" (3cm) loops at the bottom. Run needle and yarn tail back through these loops to connect them, forming pointy spikes.

Before tying off the yellow thread, make a French knot nostril on either side of the nose. Make 2 more French knots with blue yarn for the eyes. Stitch a long red mouth on either side with red yarn. Weave in ends.

TO FINISH THE HORSE

EARS

Using orange yarn, pick up and knit 3 sts on the top of the head.

Knit 1 row.

NEXT ROW: K1, k2tog—2 sts.

K2tog and fasten off.

Rep on the other side for second Ear.

MANE

With brown yarn, pick up and knit 11 sts from one side of the Horse's neck. (See page 155 in the Glossary for instructions on picking up sts.)

Knit 1 row. BO.

Rep the process on the other side of the neck; be sure to line up the second side of the Mane with the first. With yarn

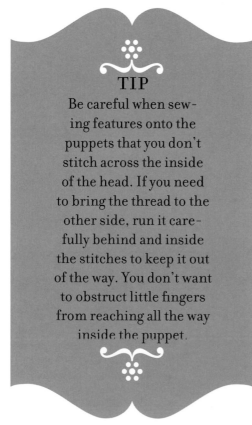

TIP

Be careful when sewing features onto the puppets that you don't stitch across the inside of the head. If you need to bring the thread to the other side, run it carefully behind and inside the stitches to keep it out of the way. You don't want to obstruct little fingers from reaching all the way inside the puppet.

tail threaded on needle, weave yarn through both sides of Mane, connecting them as you weave in your ends. Use more brown yarn to make French knots for the nostrils and a small mouth. Switch to green yarn to make 2 French knots for the eyes. Weave in ends.

PEOPLE PUPPETS

Note: All the people are made the same way except for the Queen. Just change colors and add embellishments to distinguish them from each other.

With 2 circular needles, or with DPNs, and clothing color, CO 8 sts. Join for working in the rnd, taking care not to twist sts. Work in St st for 7 rnds.

**Change to face color and work 2 rnds, then only half of the third rnd: this makes 3 rows of face color in the front, and only 2 in the back.

Change to hair color and work 2 rnds, then only half of the third rnd: this makes 3 rows of hair color in the back, and only 2 in front.

If making a hat, change colors again and knit 2 rnds.

DECREASE FOR TOP:

NEXT RND: K2tog around—4 sts.

NEXT RND: K2tog around—2 sts.

K2tog and fasten off. Weave in ends.

Use contrasting colors to embroider French knot eyes, and backstitch to make a mouth.

KING PUPPET

CROWN
Crochet a chain 4" (10cm) long and sew around the head in points, as for Dragon's tail.

CAPE
With yellow yarn, pick up and knit 5 sts across the King's back.

Knit 2 rows.

INC ROW: K1, m1, knit to last st, m1, k1—7 sts.

Knit 2 rows.

Rep Inc Row—9 sts.

Knit 1 row. BO.

JESTER PUPPET

HAT
Crochet a chain 8" (20cm) long. Sew around the head in points, as for Dragon's tail. Make French knot bells in contrasting color at the end of each point.

QUEEN PUPPET
With pink yarn, CO 32 sts. Join for working in the rnd.

Knit 1 rnd, purl 1 rnd, knit 1 rnd.

NEXT RND: K2tog around—16 sts.

Knit 1 rnd.

NEXT RND: K2tog around—8 sts.

Knit 4 rnds.

Cont as for other People Puppets from **.

BRAIDS
Cut 6 4" (10cm) strands of hair color yarn and thread them all through the eye of a large tapestry needle. Pass the needle through the top of the Queen's head. Pull the yarn so that half the length comes out either side of the head. Divide the strands into 3 pairs and braid them. Use pink yarn to secure the braid ends in a bow. Trim the hair ¼" (6mm) from the bows.

TIARA
Crochet a chain 3" (8cm) long and sew it around the front of the head in points, as for Dragon's tail.

ROYAL FELTED SLIPPERS + CROWNS

WE ALL KNOW WHO THE REAL RULERS OF OUR HOMES ARE, SO WE MIGHT AS WELL HAVE FUN CROWNING OUR LITTLE KINGS AND QUEENS IN STYLISH KNITWEAR. Unlike plastic and cardboard crowns, this soft version has a small elastic panel so it's comfortable to wear. It's sure to become one of the most popular items in your little ruler's dress-up box. Continue the royal treatment and keep their little toes warm in these stylish slippers. The slipper pattern pieces are simply cut from a large felted rectangle. (Thank you, Yvonne Naanep, for that fine sewing idea.) Sew the pieces together with colorful lengths of suede and top them with colorful buttons. To prevent slipping, apply dimensional paint to the soles of the finished slippers.

KNITTING SKILLS

garter st [garter stitch]: Knit every row

k2tog [knit 2 together]: Dec by knitting 2 sts tog as 1 st (see page 14)

St st [Stockinette stitch]: Knit on right side, purl on wrong side

Sizes

The slippers sample as pictured and the pattern as written are for a child's size 5 shoe. See page 111 for instructions on making slippers for additional sizes.

The crown is one-size-fits-all. Simply adjust the length of the elastic at the back of the crown to fit your little one's noggin.

Finished Measurements

Slippers as shown measure 6" (15cm) from heel to toe, 3¾" (10cm) high at heel, 3" (8cm) high at instep, 1" (3cm) high at toe, and 2½" (6cm) wide at opening.

Yarn

2 skeins Berroco Hip-Hop (wool, 76 yds [70m] per 100g skein) in color #7237 Way Cool or in color #7261 Blu-Dep

small amounts of Berroco Suede (nylon, 120 yds [111m] per 50g skein) in color #3753 Belle Star, in color #3786 Aloe Vera, and in color #3789 Nelly Belle (or just use Aloe Vera) for embroidery

Needles

size US 15 (10mm) straight needles

Notions

decorative buttons

dimensional fabric paint (Tulip)

pins

yarn needle

¾" (2cm) elastic

Gauge

10 sts and 12 rows = 4" (10cm) in St st, before felting

CROWN

BASE
CO 45 sts. Work 6 rows in garter st.

POINTS (MAKE 5)
For each point, work on next 9 sts, leaving rem sts on a holder. You will need to rejoin yarn before working points 2–5.

POINTY VERSION
Knit 2 rows.

NEXT ROW: K2tog, knit to last 2 sts, k2tog—7 sts.

Rep last 3 rows twice more—3 sts.

NEXT ROW: K2tog, k1—2 sts.

K2tog and fasten off.

ROUNDED VERSION
Knit 6 rows.

NEXT ROW: K2tog, knit to last 2 sts, k2tog—7 sts.

Knit 4 rows. BO.

FINISHING AND FELTING
Weave in ends, using tails to strengthen the connections between points.

Place Crown in a zippered pillowcase. Machine wash twice in warm water with mild detergent. Stretch, shape and flatten while wet and allow to dry.

Use Suede yarn (Aloe Vera) to attach buttons and embroider designs on the front of the Crown. Cut a 2" (5cm) length of elastic and sew it to the ends of the crown, adjusting to fit as necessary.

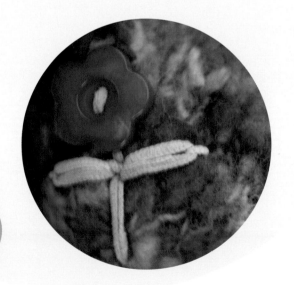

SLIPPERS

CO 30 sts. Work in St st until you've nearly used up the whole ball of yarn. BO. Felt piece and let dry (see Crown Finishing instructions, page 110).

Note: To make a very tiny pair of Slippers, you only need half a ball of yarn, but anything much larger than a size 5 Slipper will require 1 entire ball.

ASSEMBLY

Enlarge the templates until they are just the size of the child's foot, or just a bit larger (just ⅜" [9mm] will be plenty, as the fabric stretches, and too much extra fabric will cause the slipper to fall off the child's foot). Use templates to cut out slipper pieces: 1 of each piece, and 1 of each piece reversed (for right and left feet).

Place the 2 sides of 1 slipper together, right sides facing, and overcast heel and toe seams with Belle Star Suede. Sew over the heel seam a second time for reinforcement.

Turn upper right-side-out and join to sole: position the toe seam over the center top of the toe and pin. Match the heel seam to the center back of the heel and pin. Join the sides to the sole with a simple running stitch all around. Overcast this seam.

Overcast around top edge of Slipper. Sew button to front of Slipper and add embroidery if desired.

Apply lines of fabric paint to sole (to prevent slipping) and allow to dry overnight.

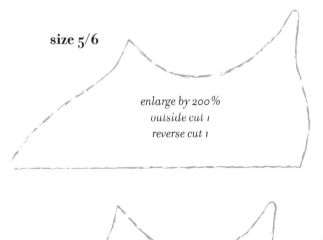

size 5/6

enlarge by 200%
outside cut 1
reverse cut 1

enlarge by 200%
inside cut 1
reverse cut 1

enlarge to size of child's foot plus ⅜" (9mm)
cut 1 for right foot
reverse cut 1 for left foot

PUP + Cat Pocket scarf + matching hat sets

IT'S SNOWING CATS AND DOGS! Make staying warm a game with this playful scarf set. If your child has a tendency to lose mittens, this scarf might be the perfect backup solution. The pockets at each end not only keep fingers warm, but will also entertain friends and passersby. Poof is so soft and bulky it takes only twelve stitches to span the width of the scarf, making this an ideal project to knit up as a gift set.

Sizes
3–6 yrs

Finished Measurements
Dog scarf: approx 42" (107cm) long
Cat scarf: approx 40" (102cm) long
Hat circumference: 18" (46cm)

Yarn

CAT
2 skeins Crystal Palace Poof (nylon microfiber, 47 yds [43m] per 50g skein) in color #9562 Red Orchid (MC)
1 skein Crystal Palace Poof in color #4649 Tea Rose (CC)

DOG
2 skeins Crystal Palace Poof in color #9374 Berry Parfait (MC),
1 skein Crystal Palace Poof in color #4650 Periwinkle (CC)

Needles
16" (40cm) size US 11 (8mm) circular needle
OR 1 set of 5 size US 11 (8mm) DPNs
1 set of 5 size US 13 (9mm) DPNs
2 size US 13 (9mm) circular needles

KNITTING SKILLS

garter st [garter stitch]: Knit every row

k2tog [knit 2 together]: Dec by knitting 2 sts tog as 1 st (see page 14)

m1 [make 1]: Inc by picking up the bar between 2 sts from front to back, place it on the left-hand needle, then knit it through the back loop (see page 15)

pm [place marker]: Slide a marker onto the needle as indicated

sm [slip marker]: Slide a marker from 1 needle to the other as indicated

St st [Stockinette stitch]: Knit on right side, purl on wrong side; when working in the rnd, knit every row

Notions
2 ⅞" (22mm) round buttons for eyes for each scarf
2 ¾" (19mm) oblong button for nose for each scarf
yarn needle

Gauge
8 sts and 11 rows = 4" (10cm) in St st with larger needles

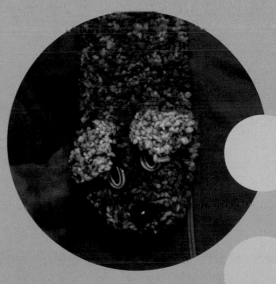

CAT (DOG) SCARF

PUPPET END

With straight needles and CC, CO 14 sts. Knit 4 rows.

DEC ROW: K2tog, knit to last 2 sts, k2tog—12 sts.

Knit 2 (3) rows.

Rep last 3 (4) rows once more—10 sts.

Rep Dec Row—8 sts.

Knit 2 (8) rows. Rep Dec Row—6 sts.

Knit 2 (3) rows. Change to MC and knit 2 (3) rows.

INC ROW: K1, m1, knit to last st, m1, k1—8 sts.

Knit 2 (8) rows. Rep Inc Row—10 sts.

Knit 2 (3) rows. Rep Inc Row—12 sts.

Knit 4 rows. Rep Inc Row—14 sts.

Knit 3 rows. Rep Dec Row—12 sts.

CENTER

Work even in garter st until Scarf measures 36" (91cm).

PUPPET END

NEXT ROW: K1, m1, knit to last st, m1, k1—14 sts.

Knit 4 rows.

DEC ROW: K2tog, knit to last 2 sts, k2tog—12 sts.

Knit 2 (3) rows. Rep Dec Row—10 sts.

Knit 2 (8) rows. Rep Dec Row—8 sts.

Knit 2 (3) rows. Change to CC and knit 2 (3) rows. Rep Dec Row—6 sts.

114

Knit 2 (8) rows.

Rep Inc Row—8 sts.

Knit 2 (3) rows.

Rep last 3 (4) rows once more—10 sts.

Rep Inc Row—12 sts.

Knit 4 rows. Rep Inc Row—14 sts.

Knit 3 rows. BO all sts.

CAT EARS (MAKE 4)
With CC and smaller needle, CO 6 sts. Knit 4 rows.

NEXT ROW: K2tog, k4—5 sts.

Knit 1 row.

NEXT ROW: K3, k2tog—4 sts.

K2tog and fasten off.

DOG EARS (MAKE 4)
With CC and smaller needle, CO 8 sts. Knit 4 rows.

NEXT ROW: K2tog, k6—7 sts.

Knit 3 rows.

NEXT ROW: K4, k2tog—6 sts.

Knit 2 rows. BO all sts.

FINISHING
On each Puppet End, fold CC section under MC and stitch sides together. Leave cast-on or bound-off edge unsewn to create a pocket for little fingers.

Attach buttons for eyes and nose. Sew Ears on. Weave in ends.

HAT
With smaller needle and CC, CO 36 sts. Join for working in the rnd. Pm for beg of rnd.

RND 1: Work in k2, p2 rib for 18 sts, pm, cont in rib to end.

Cont in k2, p2 rib for 7 more rnds.

Change to larger circular needles (or DPNs) and MC. Work in St st for 3 rnds.

NEXT RND: *K2tog, knit to marker, sm; rep from * once—34 sts.

NEXT RND: Knit.

Rep last 2 rnds 3 times more—28 sts.

NEXT RND: *K2tog, k5; rep from * to end—24 sts.

Knit 1 rnd.

NEXT RND: *K2tog, k4; rep from * to end—20 sts.

Knit 1 rnd.

NEXT RND: *K2tog, k3; rep from * to end—16 sts.

Knit 1 rnd.

NEXT RND: *K2tog, k2; rep from * to end—12 sts.

Knit 1 rnd.

NEXT RND: *K2tog, k1; rep from * to end—8 sts.

Break yarn, draw through rem sts and fasten off. Weave in ends.

BATH TIME FUN WASHCLOTHS

If your cherub cringes at the sight of a warm sudsy washcloth coming her way, it's time to knit up these intarsia patterns. The distraction of a quacking duck and spouting whale will make getting through bath time a pleasure. I was a little skeptical about knitted washcloths until I started working with this Tencel yarn and felt the buttery softness of the finished piece. And the simple single-color change makes this a great project for getting your feet wet with intarsia.

KNITTING SKILLS

garter st [garter stitch]: Knit every row

intarsia: Work in a two-color pattern by picking up a new color and twisting it around the other color at the back of the work (see page 18)

pm [place marker]: Slide a marker onto the needle as indicated

St st [Stockinette stitch]: Knit on right side, purl on wrong side

Finished Measurements

approx 9½" (24cm) square

Yarn

1 skein each of Cascade Yarns Pima Tencel (pima cotton/Tencel blend, 109 yds [100m] per 50g skein) in color #1694 royal blue (A) and color #0258 lemon (B)

several yards [meters] of Cascade Pima Tencel in color #3183 orange (C)

1 skein each of yellow and blue makes both cloths.

Needles

size US 7 (4.5mm) straight needles

Notions

stitch markers
yarn needle

Gauge

20 sts and 26 rows = 4" (10cm) in St st

Note: When working chart patterns, twist yarns together at color changes to prevent gaps. (See page 18 in the Learning the Basics section for step-by-step instructions on this technique.)

DUCK

With yarn A, CO 50 sts.

Work 10 rows in garter st. On 10th row, pm after first 10 and before last 10 sts.

NEXT ROW (RS): Work in garter st to marker, work first row of Duck Chart over center 30 sts in St st, work in garter st to end.

Cont as est, keeping 10 sts at each edge in garter st and center in St st, through end of Chart. Remove markers.

Work 10 rows in garter st.

BO all sts.

WHALE

With yarn B, CO 50 sts and work as for Duck cloth, substituting Whale Chart.

FINISHING

Weave in ends, taking care to weave yellow ends behind yellow area of knitting and blue behind blue.

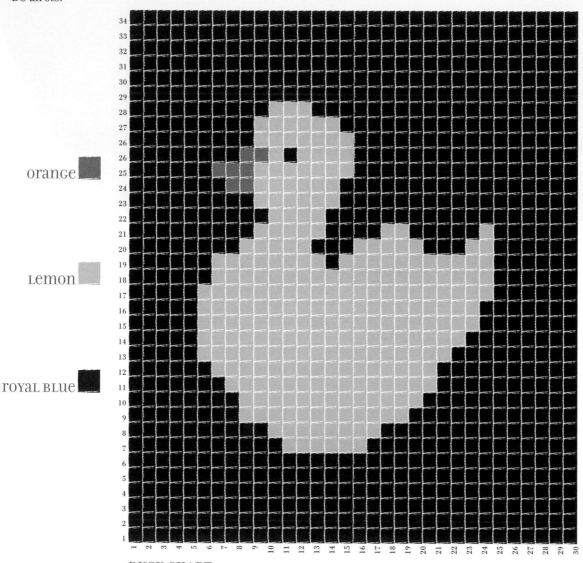

orange

lemon

royal blue

DUCK CHART

118

WHALE CHART

FOXY STOLES

REST ASSURED, NO ANIMALS WERE
HARMED IN THE MAKING OF THESE
POLITICALLY CORRECT FAUX FUR WRAPS.
Even girls who refuse to wear scarves won't hesitate
even a moment before wrapping a fuzzy fox around
their necks. This stole offers far more than mere
practical warmth—it's also a portable stuffed animal
and a dress-up accessory, all wrapped into a simple
two-skein project. Don't stop with just one, you
might know a few adults who would also fancy a
foxy stole!

KNITTING SKILLS

kfb [knit 1 front and back]: Inc by knitting 1 in the front
and back of the next st (see page 15)

k2tog [knit two together]: Dec by knitting 2 sts tog as 1 st
(see page 14)

pm [place marker]: Slide a marker onto the needle
as indicated

St st [Stockinette stitch]: Knit on right side, purl on
wrong side; when working in the rnd, knit every row

Size
for a child approx 3–6 yrs old

Finished Measurements
approx 36" (91cm) long

Yarn
2 skeins Crystal Palace Kiddo (100% nylon, 97
yds [88m] per 50g) in color #214 Pumpkin or
color #201 Almond

Needles
12" (30cm) size US 13 (9mm) circular
needle (or DPNs)
size US 10 (6mm) straight needles

Notions
1 button for nose

yarn needle

2 toggle buttons or foil-backed faceted
buttons for eyes

Gauge
9 sts and 12 rows = 4" (10cm) in St st with 2
strands held together and larger needles

NOSE

You'll start the Fox at the Nose, which is worked flat then folded and sewn together at the very end.

With 2 strands of yarn held together and smaller needles, CO 4 sts. Purl 1 row.

INC ROW (RS): Kfb, knit to last st, kfb—6 sts.

Work 3 rows even in St st.

NEXT ROW: Rep Inc Row—8 sts.

Cont in St st, rep Inc Row on every foll RS row 11 times more—30 sts. Purl 1 row.

EARS

BO 10 sts at beg of next 2 rows—10 sts. Work 4 rows even, ending with a WS row.

NECK

At this point, reverse the fabric so the Head is worked in reverse St st and the rest of the Body is worked in St st.

Change to larger needles.

NEXT ROW (WS): Purl.

NEXT ROW: Rep Inc Row from Nose directions—12 sts.

Rep last 2 rows 9 times more—30 sts.

BODY

Join for working in the rnd. Pm for beg of rnd. Work even for 5½" (14cm).

K2tog at beg of next 8 rnds—22 sts.

Return to working back and forth in rows. Cont in St st, k2tog at beg of next 14 rows—8 sts.

TAIL

Change to smaller needles. Purl 1 WS row.

NEXT ROW: Rep Inc Row (from Nose directions).

Rep last 2 rows 5 times more—20 sts.

Work 7 rows even.

DEC ROW (RS): K2tog, knit to last 2 sts, k2tog—18 sts.

NEXT ROW: Purl.

Rep last 2 rows 8 times more—2 sts.

K2tog and fasten off.

FINISHING

Fold the sides of the Fox's face in to the center, purl-side inward, and stitch them together, leaving the top 3" (8cm) unstitched to form the Ears. You may choose to place a couple of stitches at the base of the Ears to encourage them to stand up. Sew the button eyes and nose in place. Weave in any loose ends.

FLUFFY MUFFS
+ Matching Headband

WHAT LITTLE GIRL DOESN'T LOVE A COZY MUFF? This colorful update on the traditional white muff is both practical and fun. It's also one of the easiest projects in the book. If you haven't knitted in the round, this is the perfect place to get started. Fluffy Zap yarn not only adds warmth, it also conceals any uneven stitches. It's knitted along with naturally stretchy Pure Merino so little fingers can wiggle around in the warmth. Also check out the variation muff with a close-fitting ribbed cuff to keep out serious cold. If you like, use your leftovers to make a stylish matching headband. The fluffy center will keep little ears warm without creating the dreaded hat head.

KNITTING SKILLS

m1 [make 1]: Inc by picking up the bar between 2 sts from front to back, place it on the left-hand needle, then knit it through the back loop (see page 15)

p2tog [purl 2 together]: Dec by purling 2 sts tog as 1 st, just as for k2tog

St st [Stockinette stitch]: Knit on right side, purl on wrong side; when working in the rnd, knit every row

Notions

buttons or beads for flower centers (optional)

crochet hook

yarn needle

Finished Measurements

Muff: 9" (23cm) around x 10" (25cm) long

Cuffed muff: 9" (23cm) around x 16" (41cm) long

Headband: approx 17" (43cm) around

Gauge

11 sts and 16 rows = 4" (10cm) in St st, with 1 strand of MC and 2 strands of CC held together

Yarn

1 skein Berroco Pure Merino (merino wool, 92 yds [84m] per 50g skein) in color #8552 Wild Berry (purple) or in color #8517 Bluebell (lt blue) (MC)

2 skeins Berroco Zap Colors (polyester, 50 yds [46m] per 50g skein) in color #3452 Evolution (greens and purples) or in color #3461 Blu-Dep (blues and purples) (CC)

1 skein of MC is sufficient for both Muff and Headband, or for Cuffed Muff only.

Needles

2 size US 10 (6mm) circular needles

OR 1 set of 5 size US 10 (6mm) DPNs

MUFF

With 1 strand of MC and 2 strands of CC held together, CO 24 sts. Divide evenly over 2 circular needles or over DPNs and join for working in the rnd, taking care not to twist sts. (See page 16 in the Learning the Basics section for step-by-step instructions on working in the rnd with 2 circular needles.) Work in St st until Muff measures 10" (25cm). BO all sts.

FINISHING

With MC, crochet a chain 14" (36cm) long. (See page 21 in the Learning the Basics section for step-by-step instructions on crocheting a chain.) Loop the crochet chain into a flower shape and stitch it to the Muff. Add a bead or button to the center of the flower (optional). Weave in ends.

CUFFED MUFF

With MC, CO 24 sts. Divide evenly over 2 circular needles or over DPNs and join for working in the rnd, taking care not to twist sts. Work in k1, p1 rib for 3" (8cm).

Join 2 strands of CC and cont in St st with 3 strands of yarn held together for 10" (25cm). Break CC.

Work in k1, p1 rib with MC for 3" (8cm). BO all sts.

HEADBAND

With MC, CO 9 sts.

ROW 1 (RS): K1, p1, k1, p3, k1, p1, k1.

ROW 2 (WS): P1, k1, p1, k3, p1, k1, p1.

Note: 3 sts on either side of the Headband are knitted with a single strand of MC; the center sts are knitted with both MC and a single strand of CC. Let the CC strand hang while knitting the edges and simply pick it up and add it to the merino when knitting the center of the Headband.

ROW 3: K1, p1, k1, p3 with CC, k1, p1, k1.

ROW 4: P1, k1, p1, k3 with CC, p1, k1, p1.

ROWS 5–8: Rep Rows 3–4 twice more.

ROW 9: K1, p1, k1, m1 with CC, p3 with CC, m1 with CC, k1, p1, k1—11 sts.

ROW 10: P1, k1, p1, k5 with CC, p1, k1, p1.

ROW 11: K1, p1, k1, p5 with CC, k1, p1, k1.

ROW 12: P1, k1, p1, k5 with CC, p1, k1, p1.

ROWS 13–16: Rep Rows 11–12 twice more.

ROW 17: K1, p1, k1, m1 with CC, p5 with CC, m1 with CC, k1, p1, k1—13 sts.

ROW 18: P1, k1, p1, k7 with CC, p1, k1, p1.

CENTER

NEXT ROW (RS): K1, p1, k1, p7 with CC, k1, p1, k1.

NEXT ROW (WS): P1, k1, p1, k7 with CC, p1, k1, p1.

Rep last 2 rows until piece measures 14" (36cm), ending with a WS row.

END

ROW 1 (RS): K1, p1, k1, p2tog with CC, p3 with CC, p2tog with CC, k1, p1, k1—11 sts.

ROW 2 (WS): P1, k1, p1, k5 with CC, p1, k1, p1.

ROW 3: K1, p1, k1, p5 with CC, k1, p1, k1.

ROW 4: P1, k1, p1, k5 with CC, p1, k1, p1.

ROWS 5–8: Rep Rows 3–4 twice more.

ROW 9: K1, p1, k1, p2tog with CC, p1 with CC, p2tog with CC, k1, p1, k1—9 sts.

ROW 10: P1, k1, p1, k3 with CC, p1, k1, p1.

ROW 11: K1, p1, k1, p3 with CC, k1, p1, k1.

ROW 12: P1, k1, p1, k3 with CC, p1, k1, p1.

ROWS 13–16: Rep Rows 11–12 twice more.

Break CC.

ROW 17: K1, p1, k1, p3, k1, p1, k1.

ROW 18: P1, k1, p1, k3, p1, k1, p1.

BO all sts.

FINISHING

Thread a needle through the MC yarn tail and use it to join the cast-on and bound-off sts together to complete your Headband. Weave in any other loose ends. Use MC scraps to make crochet chain flowers as for Muff.

Funky Leg Warmers + Hair Scrunchie

HELP YOUR LITTLE HIP-HOP DANCER PUT HER BEST FOOT FORWARD. Leg warmers are coming back in style, and for good reason. They're a practical way to keep those little tight-clad legs warm traveling to and from cold weather dance classes. No matter how wild and crazy their dance moves, elastic yarn will hold these flashy warmers in place. And if you don't want to waste even a few yards of that special novelty yarn, transform your scraps into a unique hair elastic that will stand heads above store-bought counterparts. You get stretch from simply trapping elastic in the center of an I-cord knit in Squiggle.

KNITTING SKILLS

I-cord: Knit a tube with 2 DPNs by knitting only 1 side of the work (see page 17)

k2tog [knit two together]: Dec by knitting 2 sts tog as 1 st (see page 14)

m1 [make 1]: Inc by picking up the bar between 2 sts from front to back, place it on the left-hand needle, then knit it through the back loop (see page 15)

St st [Stockinette stitch]: Knit on right side, purl on wrong side; when working in the rnd, knit every row

Sizes
Leg warmers: S/M (M/L)

Finished Measurements
Leg warmers calf circumference: approx. 8 (9)" [20 (23)cm]

Yarn
2 (2) skeins Crystal Palace Meringue (merino wool/acrylic/elastic nylon blend, 123 yds [112m] per 50g skein) in color #9812 Violets (MC)

1 (1) skein Crystal Palace Squiggle (nylon/polyester blend, 100 yds [91m] per 50g skein) in #5182 Orchid Bloom (CC)

Note: wind Squiggle into 2 similar-sized balls so you can knit with a double strand.

Needles
1 set of 5 size US 8 (5mm) DPNs
1 set of 5 size US 10 (6mm) DPNs

Notions
child's coated hair elastic (for Scrunchie)
yarn needle

Gauge
20 sts and 30 rows = 4" (10cm) in St st with MC and smaller needles

LEGWARMERS

With smaller DPNs and MC, CO 30 (36) sts. Join for working in the rnd, being careful not to twist sts. (See page 16 in the Learning the Basics section for step-by-step instructions on working in the rnd with 2 circular needles.) Work in k1, p1 rib for 16 rnds.

Change to St st and knit 1 rnd.

NEXT RND: K1, m1, knit to end—31 (37) sts.

Knit 3 rnds.

Rep last 4 rnds 8 times more—39 (45) sts.

Work even until piece measures 8 (9)" [20 (23) cm] from cast-on edge.

NEXT RND: K1, k2tog, knit to end—38 (44) sts.

Knit 3 rnds. Rep last 4 rnds 4 times more—34 (40) sts.

Join 2 strands of CC and begin working together with MC (knitting with a total of 3 strands at once). Purl 10 rnds. Break CC.

BO loosely. Weave in ends.

HAIR SCRUNCHIE

With larger needles and 2 strands of CC held together, CO 4 sts.

Slide the sts back down to the other end of the needle and place the needle tip through the hair elastic. Knit the sts, trapping the elastic in the center of the newly formed I-cord. Cont knitting an I-cord, lifting the elastic over the knitting each time you start a new row. Once you reach halfway around the elastic, it will become harder to lift it over the knitting. When this happens, pass the yarn balls through the center of the elastic before knitting each row. Cont working in this fashion until the I-cord tube completely conceals the elastic. Before binding off, stretch the covered elastic between your fingertips: if it can expand and contract fully you're finished. Bind off, leave a tail and use it to connect the bound-off edge to the cast-on edge. To fluff up your finished Hair Band, use your needle point to pull out any fluffy squiggles that may be trapped inside the I-cord. (See page 17 in the Learning the Basics section for step-by-step instructions on knitting an I-cord.)

TIP
We use our legwarmers for everyday wear under short skirts. Knit them with elastic and novelty yarn that complement your child's wardrobe, and she can wear them every day.

WILD THINGS

YOU MAKE MY HEART SING…With faces that only a mom or child could love, these one-of-a-kind creatures are loaded with personality. Their big shiny eyes, shaggy bodies and long, flexible limbs are fascinating for little fingers to explore. Consider creating your very own wild thing. Switch colors halfway up the body, make both its arms and legs long, or how about adding a third leg? There's no wrong way to create a lovable misfit.

KNITTING SKILLS

garter st [garter stitch]: Knit every row

k2tog [knit 2 together]: Dec by knitting 2 sts tog as 1 st (see page 14)

kfb [knit 1 front and back]: Inc by knitting 1 in the front and back of the next st (see page 15)

pm [place marker]: Slide a marker onto the needle as indicated

sm [slip marker]: Slide a marker from one needle to the other, as indicated

St st [Stockinette stitch]: Knit on right side, purl on wrong side; when working in the rnd, knit every row

Finished Measurements
Pink Thing: approx 15" (38cm) tall
Purple Thing: approx 9" (23cm) tall

Yarn

PURPLE THING
1 skein Adriafil Stars (viscose/nylon blend, 71 yds [65m] per 50g skein) in color #106 Purple (MC)

1 skein Plymouth Yarns Jelli Beenz (acrylic/wool blend, 107 yds [97m] per 50g skein) each in color #1385 Pink (CC1) and in color #1382 Yellow (CC2)

PINK THING
1 skein Adriafil Stars (viscose/nylon blend, 71 yds [65m] per 50g skein) in color #258 Pink (MC)

1 skein Plymouth Yarns Jelli Beenz (acrylic/wool blend, 107 yds [97m] per 50g skein) each in color #1382 Yellow (CC1) and in color #3335 Green (CC2)

Note: The shade of green used in making the Pink Thing model has been discontinued. Color # given is the next best match.

Needles
2 size 5 US 9 (5.5mm) circular needles
OR 1 set of 5 size 5 US 9 (5.5mm) DPNs

Notions
1" (3cm) safety eyes (screw eyes with backing)
polyester fiberfill
stitch holders
stitch markers
yarn needle

Gauge
10 sts and 16 rows = 4" (10cm) in St st, with 2 strands of MC held together

PURPLE THING

BODY

With 2 strands of MC held together, CO 24 sts. Divide evenly over 2 circular needles or over DPNs and join for working in the rnd, taking care not to twist sts. (See page 16 in the Learning the Basics section for step-by-step instructions on working in the rnd with 2 circular needles.) Pm for beg of rnd.

RND 1: K12, pm, knit to end.

Work even in St st until piece measures 3" (8cm).

INC RND: *Kfb, knit to 1 st before marker, kfb, sm; rep from * once—26 sts.

Knit 3 rnds.

Rep last 4 rnds 3 times more—32 sts.**

EARS

NEXT RND: K3, BO 10, k6 and place these sts on holder, BO 10, k3—6 sts.

Work in the rnd on rem 6 sts for 3 rnds. Break yarn, draw through rem sts and fasten off.

Replace 6 held sts on DPN, join yarn, and complete as for first Ear.

ARMS (MAKE 2)

With CC1, CO 16 sts. Divide evenly over DPNS and join for working in the rnd, taking care not to twist sts. Work in St st for 7" (18cm).

HAND

NEXT RND: K5, k2tog, k2, k2tog, k5—14 sts.

NEXT RND: K4, k2tog, k2, k2tog, k4—12 sts.

NEXT RND: K3, k2tog, k2, k2tog, k3—10 sts.

NEXT RND: K2, k2tog, k2, k2tog, k2—8 sts.

NEXT RND: K1, k2tog, k1, k2tog, k1—6 sts.

NEXT RND: K1, k2tog, k1, k2tog—4 sts.

NEXT RND: K2tog twice—2 sts.

K2tog and fasten off.

LEGS (MAKE 2)

With CC2, CO 16 sts. Divide evenly over 2 circular needles or over DPNs and join for working in the rnd, taking care not to twist sts. Work in St st for 1½" (4cm).

FOOT

Shape as for Hand.

PINK THING

With MC, work Body as for Purple Thing to **. BO. Turn the finished Body upside down so that the wider part is on the bottom.

EARS/POINTED HEAD

With 2 strands of MC held together, pick up and knit 6 sts from one side of Head. (See page 155 in the Glossary for instructions on picking up sts.) Work 2 rows in garter st.

NEXT ROW: K2tog, k2, k2tog—4 sts.

Work 2 rows in garter st.

NEXT ROW: K2tog twice—2 sts.

BO.

Rep 3 times more, picking up 6 sts on the other side of the Head, then 6 at center front and center back.

Using a scrap of MC, sew around the 3 points to close the top of the Head. Fold the side points in half and sew them together down 1 side. Join the center points with a seam on either side.

ARMS (MAKE 2)

Work as for Purple Thing, but begin Hand after 6" (15cm) of St st.

LEGS (MAKE 2)

With CC2, CO 24 sts. Divide evenly over 2 circular needles or over DPNs and join for working in the rnd, taking care not to twist sts. Work in St st for 2" (5cm).

NEXT RND: K2tog, knit to end—23 sts.

Knit 2 rnds.

NEXT RND: Knit to last 2 sts, k2tog—22 sts.

Knit 2 rnds.

Rep last 6 rnds 3 times more—16 sts.

Work even for 2" (5cm).

Shape Foot as for Hand (see Pink Thing Hand instructions).

FINISHING (BOTH THINGS)

Turn Arms and Legs inside out so that reverse St st is on outside. Stuff Arms and Legs lightly. Stuff the Body minimally, leaving the ends open while positioning the eyes. Push the eyes through the front of the body and anchor. With MC, stitch the top of the Head closed. Add more stuffing to tightly pack the body, then stitch a stuffed Leg to either side of the base. Stitch the opening between the Legs closed. Stitch a stuffed Arm to either side of the Body. With CC1, stitch a straight seam through Arms/Legs about 3" (8cm) from the end to form a wrist or ankle.

FACE DETAILS

With CC, outline the desired shape with running stitch. Work satin stitch over the running stitch guidelines.

KNITTED MOUTH

With CC1, CO 12 sts. Knit 1 row. BO.

Use the yarn tail to stitch the mouth to the front of your Thing in a slightly curved smile.

hand puppet trio

LIONS and ELEPHANTS and MONKEYS...Oh My! There's nothing scary about these animated puppets. They're so soft, you'll want to sneak your hands inside them to bring them alive. Multiple openings allow your fingertips to move all the arms and legs, and even the elephant's tusks and trunk. Perfect for the bathtub, these puppets will stir up fun and bubbles when it's time to get clean. Just hang them up to dry—they don't like the clothes dryer. Best of all, you only need three skeins of yarn to knit up this trio.

KNITTING SKILLS

k2tog [knit two together]: Dec by knitting 2 sts tog as 1 st (see page 14)

kfb [knit 1 front and back]: Inc by knitting 1 in the front and back of the next st (see page 15)

m1 [make 1]: Inc by picking up the bar between 2 sts from front to back, place it on the left-hand needle, then knit it through the back loop (see page 15)

p2tog [purl two together]: Dec by purling 2 sts tog as 1 st, just as for k2tog

St st [Stockinette stitch]: Knit on right side, purl on wrong side; when working in the rnd, knit every row

yo [yarn over]: Wrap the yarn once around the right-hand needle and cont knitting; on the subsequent row, treat the wrap as a st, creating an eyelet hole in the knitted fabric

Finished Measurements
approx 11" (28cm) tall

Yarn
1 skein Sirdar Snuggly Confetti (74% polyester, 26% nylon; 82 yd [75m] per 50g skein) each in color #0810 Stone (A), in color #0809 Chino (B) and in color #0808 Playtime Blue (C)

1 skein of each color makes all 3 puppets.

scraps of different colors of worsted weight yarn for faces

Needles
2 size US 10½ (6.5mm) circular needles OR 1 set of 5 size US 10½ (6.5mm) DPNs

Notions
stitch holder

yarn needle

Gauge
14 sts and 12 rows = 4" (10cm) in St st

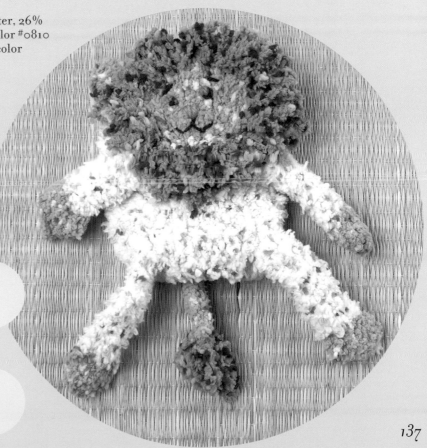

ELEPHANT

BODY

With yarn C, CO 30 sts. Divide evenly over 2 circular needles or over DPNs and join for working in the rnd, taking care not to twist sts. (See page 16 in the Learning the Basics section for step-by-step instructions on working in the rnd with 2 circular needles.) The beg of the rnd is at the side of the puppet. Work 1" (3cm) in St st.

FRONT AND BACK LEG OPENINGS

NEXT RND: *K2, k2tog, yo, k7, yo, k2tog, k2; rep from * once.

Knit 2 rnds.

TAIL OPENING

NEXT RND: K22, yo, k2tog, k6.

Knit 10 rnds.

DIVIDE FRONT AND BACK OF HEAD

NEXT RND: K15. Place rem 15 sts for back of head on holder. *Begin working from chart.

FRONT OF HEAD

TUSK OPENINGS

NEXT ROW (WS): P3, p2tog, yo, p5, yo, p2tog, p3.

Work 2 rows even.

TRUNK OPENING

NEXT ROW (RS): P6, BO 3, p6.

NEXT ROW (WS): K6, CO 3, k6.

Work 7 rows even.

**SHAPE TOP OF HEAD:

NEXT ROW (RS): K2tog, knit to last 2 sts, k2tog—13 sts.

NEXT ROW (WS): P2tog, purl to last 2 sts, p2tog—11 sts.

Rep last 2 rows once more—7 sts.

BO.**

BACK OF HEAD

Replace 15 held sts on needle and rejoin yarn C. Purl 1 WS row.

EARS

ROW 1 (RS): CO 3 sts, k15, CO 3 sts—21 sts.

ROW 2 (WS): P1, m1, purl to last st, m1, p1—23 sts.

ROW 3: K1, m1, knit to last st, m1, k1—25 sts.

ROW 4: Rep Row 2—27 sts.

ROW 5: (K1, m1) twice, knit to last 2 sts, (m1, k1) twice—31 sts.

Work 5 rows even.

BO 4 sts at beg of next 4 rows—15 sts.

Shape top as for Front of Head from ** to **.

Stitch the Back and Front of the Head together, letting Ear flaps extend out to the sides.

TRUNK

With yarn C, pick up and knit 10 sts around Trunk opening. (See page 155 in the Glossary for instructions on picking up sts.) Join for working in the rnd. Work in St st for 3" (8cm). BO.

TUSKS (MAKE 2)

With yarn B, pick up and knit 4 sts around Tusk opening. Join for working in the rnd.

Work in St st for 1¾" (4cm).

NEXT RND: K2tog around—2 sts.

K2tog and fasten off.

TAIL

With yarn C, pick up and knit 4 sts around Tail opening. Join for working in the rnd. Work in St st 2½" (6cm).

NEXT RND: K2tog around—2 sts.

K2tog and fasten off.

With yarn B threaded on tapestry needle, sew 4 1½" (4cm) long loops to end of Tail.

LEGS (MAKE 4)

With yarn C, pick up and knit 12 sts around Leg Opening. Join for working in the rnd. Work in St st for 3" (8cm). Change to yarn B and knit 1 row. BO.

FINISHING

FACE

With a double strand of orange yarn, embroider an elongated v-shaped mouth under the trunk. Then make 2 round eyes above the trunk. Make 2 French knot pupils with brown yarn, and 2 eyebrows with a double strand of pink yarn.

Weave in ends.

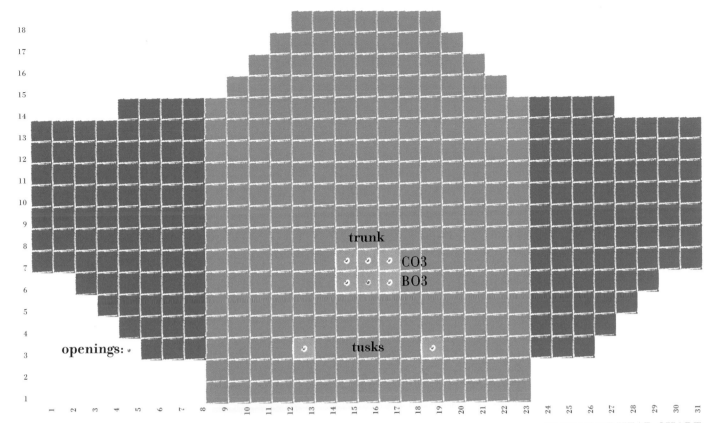

ELEPHANT HEAD CHART

trunk

CO3

BO3

openings:

tusks

ADDED STS FOR EARS

OPENINGS FOR FRONT ONLY

KNIT THE SAME FOR FRONT
AND BACK OF HEAD

139

MONKEY

BODY

With yarn A, CO 26 sts. Divide evenly over 2 circular needles or over DPNs and join for working in the rnd, taking care not to twist sts. (See page 16 in the Learning the Basics section for step-by-step instructions on working in the rnd with 2 circular needles.) The beg of the rnd is at the side of the puppet.

Work 1" (3cm) in St st.

BACK LEG OPENINGS

NEXT RND: K15, k2tog, yo, k5, yo, k2tog, knit to end.

Knit 2 rnds.

TAIL OPENING

NEXT RND: K19, yo, k2tog, k5.

Knit 8 rnds.

FRONT LEG OPENINGS

NEXT RND: K2, k2tog, yo, k5, yo, k2tog, knit to end.

Knit 2 rnds.

DIVIDE FRONT AND BACK OF HEAD

NEXT RND: K13. Place rem 13 sts for Back of Head on holder.**

FRONT OF HEAD

Follow the Monkey Head Chart to add a contrast-color face to your puppet. Be sure to follow the top of the head shaping instructions marked on the chart.

BACK OF HEAD

With MC, work 6 rows even, beg with a RS row.

NEXT ROW (RS): Join yarn B. M1 in B, k11 in A, join second strand of B, m1 in B—15 sts.

NEXT ROW: Kfb with yarn B, p13 with yarn A, kfb with yarn B—17 sts.

NEXT ROW: Kfb, k1 with yarn B, k13 with yarn A, k1, kfb with yarn B—19 sts.

NEXT ROW: P2tog, p1 with yarn B, p13 with yarn A p1, p2tog with yarn B—17 sts.

NEXT ROW: K2tog with yarn B, k13 with yarn A, k2tog with yarn B—15 sts. Break B.

NEXT ROW: P2tog, p11, p2tog—13 sts.

NEXT ROW: K2tog, k9, k2tog—11 sts.

NEXT ROW: P2tog, p7, p2tog—9 sts.

NEXT ROW: K2tog, k5, k2tog—7 sts.

BO.

Stitch the Front of the Head to the Back, letting the small ear flaps extend out the sides.

TAIL

With B, pick up and knit 8 sts around Tail opening. Join for working in the rnd.

Work in St st for 6" (15cm).

NEXT RND: K2tog, knit to end—7 sts.

Rep last rnd 3 times more—4 sts.

NEXT RND: K2tog around—2 sts.

K2tog and fasten off.

FRONT (BACK) LEGS (MAKE 2 OF EACH)

With A, pick up and knit 8 sts around leg opening. (See page 155 in the Glossary for instructions on picking up sts.) Join for working in the rnd. Work in St st for 2½ (4½)" [6 (11)cm].

Change to yarn B. Knit 3 rnds.

NEXT RND: K2tog around—4 sts.

NEXT RND: K2tog around—2 sts.

K2tog and fasten off.

FINISHING

FACE

Make 2 large French knot eyes with a double strand of green yarn. With pink yarn make a w-shaped mouth, work satin stitch vertically to create a nose with brown yarn, then stitch 2 vertical pupils across each eye.

Weave in ends.

LION

With yarn B, work as for Monkey to **.

FRONT OF HEAD

Follow the Head Chart to add a contrast-color face to your puppet. Be sure to follow the top of the head shaping instructions marked on the chart.

BACK OF HEAD

Replace 13 held sts on needle. Work 10 rows in St st, beg with a WS row.

NEXT ROW (RS): Join yarn A, CO 2 with yarn A, k13 with yarn B, join second strand of yarn A, CO 2 in A—17 sts.

LION + MONKEY HEAD CHART
Reverse Monkey or Lion Ear and repeat on
other side of Puppet's Head to make second Ear.

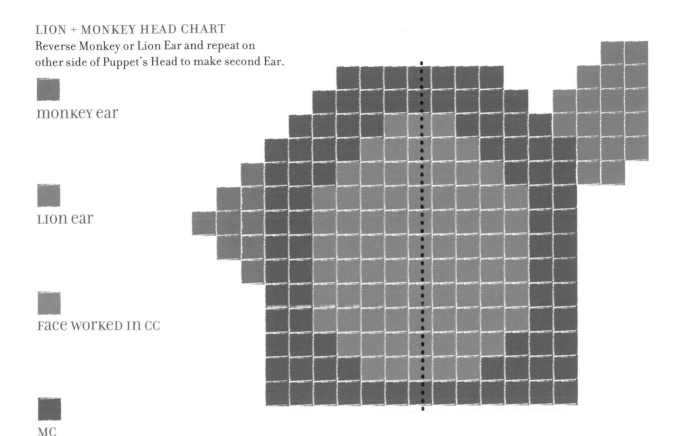

■ monkey ear

■ lion ear

■ face worked in CC

■ MC

NEXT ROW (WS): Kfb, p1 with yarn A, p13 with yarn B, p1,
kfb with yarn A—19 sts.

NEXT ROW: K4 with yarn A, k11 with yarn B, k4 with
yarn A.

NEXT ROW: P4 with yarn A, BO 1 with yarn B, p9 with yarn
A, BO 1 with yarn A, p4 with yarn A—17 sts.

NEXT ROW: K2, k2tog with yarn A, k2tog, k5, k2tog with
yarn B, k2tog, k2 with yarn A—13 sts.

NEXT ROW: P1, p2tog with yarn A, BO 7 with yarn B, k2tog,
k1 with yarn A—4 sts.

NEXT ROW: BO 2 with yarn A, BO 2 with yarn A.

Stitch the front of the Head to the Back, letting the small
ear flaps extend out the top sides of the Head.

TAIL
With yarn A, pick up and knit 6 sts around Tail opening.
Join for working in the rnd. Work in St st for 4" (10cm).

NEXT RND: (K2tog, k1) twice—4 sts.

NEXT RND: K2tog twice—2 sts.

K2tog and fasten off.

With C threaded on tapestry needle, sew 8 2½" (6cm) loops
to end of Tail.

FRONT (BACK) LEGS (MAKE 2 OF EACH)
With B, pick up and knit 8 sts around Leg Opening. Join for
working in the rnd. Work in St st for 3 (4)" [8 (10)cm].

Change to C. Knit 1 rnd.

NEXT RND: Kfb, k2, kfb twice, k2, kfb—12 sts.

NEXT RND: K2tog, k2, k2tog twice, k2, k2tog—8 sts.

NEXT RND: K2tog around—4 sts.

NEXT RND: K2 tog around—2 sts.

BO.

FINISHING

FACE
Use satin stitch to create a nose with green yarn. Make 2
large French knot eyes with a double strand of pink yarn.
With brown yarn make a w-shaped mouth, stitch 2 vertical pupils across each eye and then make 2 simple single-
stitched eyebrows.

MANE
Thread a long length of yarn C through a tapestry needle.
Stitch 2 rows of 2" (5cm) loops around the Lion's face.

Weave in ends.

BULKY HAND-DYED BACKPACK + MATCHING MOM TOTE

IF YOU WANT INSTANT KNITTING GRATIFICATION, reach for a ball of chunky yarn. You'll be amazed how quickly it knits together into a substantial piece of fabric. Perfectly sized for a child's back, this backpack is great for carrying a snack, book or small toy for a short outing. This yarn knits up so quickly—you might just want to make the matching tote for a deserving mom. While this tote won't solve all the logistical problems of motherhood, it is a good size to accommodate the basics—diapers, wipes, a sippy cup, wallet, keys and cell phone—without becoming unwieldy. Both the decorative topstitching and handpainted ceramic buttons transform the simple shape into a stylish carry-all that is sure to garner compliments.

KNITTING SKILLS

garter st [garter stitch]: Knit every row

I-cord: Knit a tube with 2 DPNs by knitting only one side of the work (see page 17)

k2tog [knit two together]: Dec by knitting 2 sts tog as 1 st (see page 14)

St st [Stockinette stitch]: Knit on right side, purl on wrong side

---

Finished Measurements
Backpack: approx 10" x 7½" x 2" (25cm x 19cm x 5cm)
Tote for Mom: approx 9½" x 7½" x 2" (24cm x 19cm x 5cm)

Yarn

BACKPACK
2 skeins Blue Sky Alpacas Bulky Hand Dyes (alpaca/wool blend, 45 yds [41 m] per 100 g skein) in color #1023 Daffodil (MC)

1 skein Blue Sky Alpacas Bulky Hand Dyes in color #1020 Lilac (CC1)

a few yards Blue Sky Alpacas Sport Weight (100% baby alpaca, 110 yds [100 m] per 50 g skein) in color #531 Paprika for embroidery (CC2)

TOTE FOR MOM
2 skeins Blue Sky Alpacas Bulky Hand Dyes in color #1018 Peace Pink (MC)

1 skein Blue Sky Alpacas Bulky Hand Dyes in color #1020 Lilac (CC1)

a few yards of Blue Sky Alpacas Sport Weight in color #520 Avocado for embroidery

Needles
any length size US 15 (10mm) circular needles

Notions
1 large ceramic button for each bag
scrap yarn
yarn needle

Gauge
8 sts and 12 rows = 4" (10cm) in St st with MC, before felting

⁂ BACKPACK

BODY

With MC, CO 24 sts. Beg with a knit row, work in St st for 16 rows. At the end of 16th row, tie pieces of scrap yarn around the first and last sts on the needle.

Cont in St st for 20 rows. Tie scrap yarn around the first and last sts on the needle.

Cont in St st for 16 rows. BO in purl on RS of work.

BASE

With MC and WS facing, pick up and knit 20 sts along one side edge of Body, between markers. (See page 155 in the Glossary for instructions on picking up sts.) Work in garter st for 5 rows. BO.

TOP FLAP

With CC1 and WS facing, pick up and knit 20 sts between markers along the opposite edge of Body. Work in St st for 12 rows, beg with a knit row.

BUTTONHOLE

NEXT ROW: K9, BO 2, k9.

NEXT ROW: P9, CO 2 over gap, k9.

Work in garter st for 2 rows. BO in purl on RS.

STRAPS (MAKE 2)

With CC1, CO 6 sts. Work in I-cord for 16" (41cm). BO.

FINISHING

Weave in ends. Remove yarn markers before felting. See page 145 for information on felting.

Fold short ends of Body together. With CC and tapestry needle, stitch cast-on and bound-off edges together. Sew free edges of Base to bottom of Body. Stitch Straps to Back, positioning them close together at top and about 3½" (9cm) apart at bottom.

TOTE FOR MOM

BACK
With MC, CO 24 sts. Work 3 rows garter st. Cont in St st for 22 rows, beg with a knit row.

BASE
Change to CC1 and work 9 rows in garter st.

FRONT
Change to MC and work 18 rows in St st, beg with a knit row.

STRAP OPENING
NEXT ROW (RS): K11, BO 2, k11.

NEXT ROW (WS): P11, CO 2 sts over gap, p1.

Work 2 rows in garter st. BO in purl on RS.

SIDES (MAKE 2)
With CC1 and with RS facing, pick up and knit 6 sts from base of bag. (See page 155 in the Glossary for instructions on picking up sts.) Work in St st for 21 rows, beg with a purl row. Work 2 rows garter st. BO in purl on RS.

FRONT STRAP
With CC1, working on WS of Back, pick up and knit 4 sts at center top, just underneath the garter st edge. Work 4 rows St st, beg with a purl row.

Divide into 2 sets of 2 sts, join a second length of yarn, and work each set separately for 4 rows.

NEXT ROW (WS): Purl across all 4 sts.

NEXT ROW: K2tog twice—K2tog and fasten off.

HANDLES (MAKE 2)
With MC, CO 5 sts.

Work in St st for 15" (38cm). BO.

FINISHING

FELTING (BOTH BAGS)
Place item in a zippered pillow case and machine wash in warm water with mild detergent, checking frequently to see if item is sufficiently felted. It may take more than one trip through the wash to felt item completely. Take out of the machine and shape, and let air dry.

ASSEMBLY
Stitch the ceramic bead to the front of the bag, leaving a ¼" (6mm) shank of yarn between the purse and button, so button can maneuver easily in and out of the buttonhole.

With CC1, seam Sides to Front and Back. Attach Handles to inside of bag, stitching just below the garter st top edging. Weave in ends.

Use CC2 to overcast the seams of your finished bag.

ANIMAL APPLIQUÉ TOTES

I DESIGNED THE SQUIRREL TOTE WITH MY LITTLE CELIA IN MIND. She loves watching squirrels' antics on our walks. Sightings are a novelty as our dog's mission is to chase them into the trees. Perfectly sized for toddlers and preschoolers, either of these little totes will carry a small doll and a few little books. Try either version of the tote, and feel free to mix and match the appliquéd animals.

KNITTING SKILLS

garter st [garter stitch]: Knit every row

k2tog [knit two together]: Dec by knitting 2 sts tog as 1 st (see page 14)

kfb [knit 1 front and back]: Inc by knitting 1 in the front and back of the next st (see page 15)

m1 [make 1]: Inc by picking up the bar between 2 sts from front to back, place it on the left-hand needle, then knit it through the back loop (see page 15)

pm [place marker]: Slide a marker onto the needle as indicated to count sts

sm [slip marker]: Slide a marker from one needle to the other, as indicated

St st [Stockinette stitch]: Knit on right side, purl on wrong side; when working in the rnd, knit every row

Finished Measurements
Butterfly: approx 8" (base) x 4½" x 3" (20cm x 11cm x 8cm)
Squirrel: approx 7" (top) x 5¾" x 2" (18cm x 15cm x 5cm)

Yarn
1 skein Blue Sky Alpacas Sport Weight (100% baby alpaca, 110 yds [100m] per 50g skein) each in color #521 Tangerine (A), in color #530 Fuchsia (B), and in color #532 Turquoise (C)

2 skeins of each color will make both totes

Note: Before beginning to knit, wind each skein of yarn into 2 balls. You will work with 2 strands of yarn held together throughout.

Needles
16" (40cm) size US 10 (6mm) circular needle

Notions
stitch holders or scrap yarn
stitch markers
yarn needle

Gauge
16 sts and 20 rows = 4" (10cm) in St st before felting, with 2 strands of yarn held together

SQUIRREL TOTE

Note: Work with 2 strands of yarn held tog throughout.

BASE
With yarn A, CO 18 sts. Work in garter st for 16 rows. Do not turn work at end of last row. Change to yarn C.

NEXT ROW: Pick up and knit 8 sts from side of garter st rectangle, pm, pick up and knit 16 sts from bottom of rectangle (cast-on edge), pm, pick up and knit 8 sts from side, pm for beg of rnd—48 sts. (See page 155 in the Glossary for instructions on picking up sts.) Join for working in the rnd.

Work 4 rnds St st.

FRONT & BACK SHAPING

INC RND: *K1, m1, knit to 1 st before marker, m1, k1, sm, k8, sm; rep from * once—52 sts.

Work 4 rnds even.

Rep Inc Rnd—56 sts.

Work 2 rnds even.

Rep last 3 rnds 3 times more, then Inc Rnd once more—72 sts.

TOP EDGE
Knit 1 rnd, then purl 1 rnd.

Rep Inc Rnd—76 sts.

Purl 1 rnd, then knit 1 rnd. BO.

HANDLES
Each Handle is made with 2 separate strips that are seamed together lengthwise with wrong sides facing.

Working on front of Tote with yarn C, pick up and knit 4 sts at base of garter st edging, beg 6 sts to left of right front center. Work in St st, beg with a purl row, for 11" (28cm).

Working on front with yarn C, pick up and knit 4 sts at base of edging, ending 6 sts to right of left front corner. Work in St st, beg with a knit row, for 11" (28cm).

Lay one strip over the other, wrong sides together, and seam. Rep for back of Tote.

SQUIRREL DETAIL
With yarn A, CO 20 sts. Work 22 rows in garter st. BO. Felt this square along with the Tote. (See the Finishing/Felting instructions, below.)

After felting, cut out squirrel shape using template (see page 149). Use yarn A to stitch the squirrel to the Tote. With yarn C, embroider a French knot for the eye.

Use template to cut out an acorn from felted scraps left over from Butterfly Purse. (If not making Butterfly Purse, knit a garter st square 10 sts by 10 rows with yarn B, and felt this along with the Squirrel Tote). Attach the acorn to the Tote with yarn B. Top with cap cut from scraps of yarn A and embroider a crosshatch design over cap with yarn B. Make a single backstitch in yarn A for acorn stem.

FINISHING/FELTING (BOTH BAGS)
Weave in ends.

Place bag(s) and knitted square for Squirrel Detail in a zippered pillowcase and machine wash in warm water with mild detergent, checking progress of felting frequently. More than one wash cycle may be needed to completely felt bag. Remove bag from machine, shape, and allow to air dry.

Attach appliqués after felting (see Butterfly and Squirrel Detail instructions).

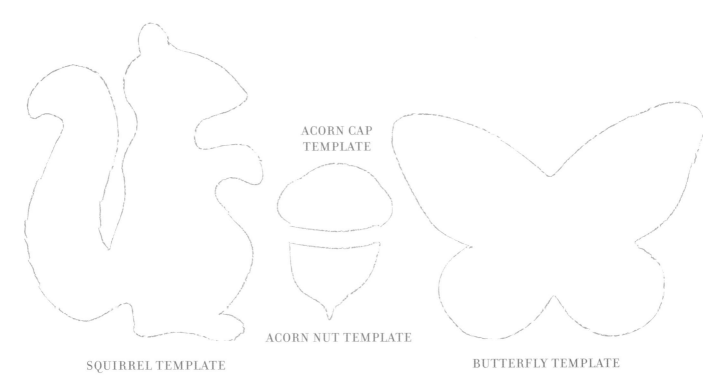

ACORN CAP
TEMPLATE

ACORN NUT TEMPLATE

SQUIRREL TEMPLATE

BUTTERFLY TEMPLATE

ALL TEMPLATES SHOWN AT 100%.

BUTTERFLY PURSE

Note: Work with 2 strands of yarn held tog throughout.

BASE

With yarn B, CO 30 sts. Work 24 rows in garter st. Do not turn work at end of last row. Change to yarn A.

NEXT ROW: Pm, pick up and knit 10 sts from side of garter st rectangle, pm, pick up and knit 30 sts from bottom of rectangle (cast-on edge), pm, pick up and knit 10 sts from side, pm for beg of rnd—80 sts. (See page 155 in the Glossary for instructions on picking up sts.)

Join for working in the rnd. Work in St st for 6 rnds.

SIDE PANEL SHAPING

NEXT RND: Knit to first marker, sm, k2tog, knit to 2 sts before second marker, k2tog, sm, knit to third marker, sm, k2tog, knit to 2 sts before last marker, k2tog—76 sts.

Knit 1 rnd.

Rep last 2 rnds twice more—68 sts.

FRONT AND BACK SHAPING

NEXT RND: *K2tog, knit to 2 sts before first marker, k2tog, sm, k4, sm; rep from * once—64 sts.

Knit 1 rnd.

Rep last 2 rnds 6 times more—40 sts.

NEXT RND: BO 16 (front of purse), place next 4 sts on a holder, k16 (back of purse), place last 4 sts on a holder.

FLAP

Working on the 16 sts of purse back, change to yarn C. Purl 1 WS row.

NEXT ROW (RS): Kfb, knit to last st, kfb—18 sts.

Knit 1 row.

Rep last 2 rows twice more—22 sts.

Cont in garter st for 6 rows.

NEXT ROW: K2tog, knit to last 2 sts, k2tog—20 sts.

Knit 1 row.

Rep last 2 rows 4 times more—12 sts.

BO.

HANDLE

With yarn B and RS facing, replace 4 sts from one holder on needle. Work in St st, beg with a knit row, for 15" (38cm). BO.

With yarn B and RS facing, replace 4 sts from second holder on needle. Work in St st, beg with a purl row, for 15" (38cm). BO.

Lay one Handle over the other, wrong sides facing, and stitch together.

BUTTERFLY DETAIL

With yarn B, CO 20 sts. Work 22 rows in garter st. BO. Felt this square along with the Tote. See the Finishing/Felting section on page 148 in the Squirrel Tote pattern for felting instructions.

After felting, cut out butterfly shape using template (see page 149). Apply the butterfly to the purse flap and stitch with yarn A along the center of the butterfly body. Use backstitch to embroider 2 antennae. Tack wings in place with yarn B.

If making Squirrel Tote, reserve felted scraps of yarn B to make squirrel's acorn.

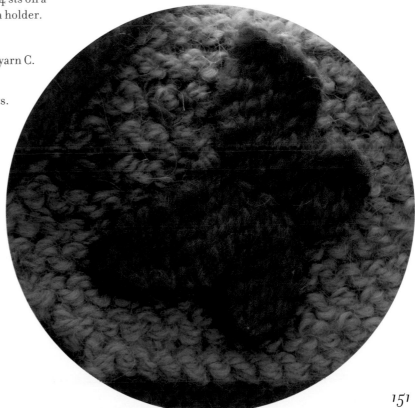

basic knitting information

KNITTING ABBREVIATIONS

beg	BEGINNING
CC	CONTRAST COLOR
CO	CAST ON
dec	DECREASE
DPN(s)	DOUBLE-POINTED NEEDLE(S)
foll	FOLLOWING
inc	INCREASE
k	KNIT
k2tog	KNIT 2 TOGETHER
kfb	KNIT 1 FRONT AND BACK
M1	MAKE ONE
MC	MAIN COLOR
p	PURL
pm	PLACE MARKER
p2tog	PURL 2 TOGETHER
psso	PASS SLIPPED STITCH OVER
rem	REMAINING
RS	RIGHT SIDE
rep	REPEAT
sl	SLIP STITCH
sm	SLIP MARKER
SSK	SLIP, SLIP, KNIT
st(s)	STITCH(ES)
work 2 tog	WORK 2 TOGETHER
WS	WRONG SIDE
yo	YARN OVER

KNITTING NEEDLE CONVERSIONS

diameter (mm)	US size	suggested yarn weight
2	0	LACE WEIGHT
2.25	1	LACE AND FINGERING WEIGHT
2.75	2	LACE AND FINGERING WEIGHT
3.25	3	FINGERING AND SPORT WEIGHT
3.5	4	FINGERING AND SPORT WEIGHT
3.75	5	DK AND SPORT WEIGHT
4	6	DK, SPORT AND ARAN/WORSTED WEIGHT
4.5	7	ARAN/WORSTED WEIGHT
5	8	ARAN/WORSTED AND HEAVY WORSTED WEIGHT
5.5	9	ARAN/WORSTED, HEAVY WORSTED AND CHUNKY/BULKY
6	10	CHUNKY/BULKY
6.5	10½	CHUNKY/BULKY AND SUPER BULKY
8	11	CHUNKY/BULKY AND SUPER BULKY
9	13	SUPER BULKY
10	15	SUPER BULKY
12.75	17	SUPER BULKY
15	19	SUPER BULKY
20	36	SUPER BULKY

yarn weight guidelines

The names given to different weights of yarn can vary widely depending on the country of origin or the yarn manufacturer's preference. The Craft Yarn Council of America has put together a standard yarn weight system to impose a bit of order on the sometimes unruly yarn labels. Look for a picture of a skein of yarn with a number 1–6 on most kinds of yarn to figure out its "official" weight. Gauge is given over Stockinette stitch. The information in the chart below is taken from www.yarnstandards.com.

	SUPER BULKY (6)	BULKY (5)	MEDIUM (4)	LIGHT (3)	FINE (2)	SUPERFINE (1)
Description	bulky, roving	chunky, craft, rug	worsted, afghan, aran	dk, light, worsted	sport, baby	sock, fingering, baby
Stitches per inch	6–11 sts	12–15 sts	16–20 sts	21–24 sts	23–26 sts	27–32 sts
Recommended needle size	11 and larger	9 to 11	7 to 9	5 to 7	3 to 5	1 to 3

substituting yarns

If you substitute yarn, be sure to select a yarn of the same weight as the yarn recommended for the project. Even after checking that the recommended gauge on the yarn you plan to substitute is the same as for the yarn listed in the pattern, make sure to swatch and see. Use the chart above as a general guideline for selecting a yarn to substitute.

❧ Glossary

CASTING ON (CO)

Casting on is the term for creating the number of stitches needed for the first row of any project. There are several methods for casting on—for the projects in this book, long-tail cast on is the most commonly used.

LONG-TAIL CAST ON

This type of cast on creates a stable, even edge. It requires only one knitting needle held in one hand and the yarn held in the other. See page 12 in the Learning the Basics section for step-by-step instructions for casting on with this technique.

BACKWARD-LOOP CAST ON

Use this method to cast on stitches in the middle of a row or in the middle of a knitted piece. This type of cast on is generally used in conjunction with one or two bound-off stitches to create a buttonhole, or to add multiple stitches at the beginning or end of a row when a dramatic increase is necessary. To cast on stitches using this method, simply make a loop with the working yarn, making sure the yarn crosses over itself on the side facing the right-hand needle. Slip the loop onto the right-hand needle and pull it snug. Continue casting on as many stitches as instructed. On the subsequent row, knit the loops just as you would regular stitches.

WITH DOUBLE-POINTED NEEDLES

If one of your double-pointed needles can accommodate the full number of stitches, cast all of the stitches onto one needle. If your needles are shorter, you may opt to cast all of the stitches onto one longer straight needle. Once all of the stitches have been cast on, divide them evenly between four of the DPN. To divide the stitches, hold the needle with the cast-on stitches in your left hand, as if to knit. Using a DPN, insert the tip of the needle into the first stitch as if to purl. Slip the stitch to the right-hand needle. Continue to slip stitches as if to purl until the stitches are divided evenly over four needles. The remaining DPN is for knitting.

COLOR WORK

INTARSIA

At each color change, yarns must be wrapped around each other at the back of the work to prevent holes in the fabric. You may work with separate skeins, with yarn wound on bobbins, or with very long strands of yarn. Take time to untangle your strands every few rows. See page 18 in the Learning the Basics section for illustrated instructions on working in intarsia.

DECREASES

KNIT TWO TOGETHER (K2TOG)

Knitting two stitches together as one (k2tog) is a simple way to decrease the number of stitches in a row. Simply slip your right-hand needle through the first two stitches on the left-hand needle from front to back, as for a regular knit stitch. Knit the two stitches as one, creating one less stitch. See page 14 in the Learning the Basics section for illustrated instructions on knitting two together.

PURL TWO TOGETHER (P2TOG)

Slip your right-hand needle through the first two stitches on the left-hand needle from back to front, as for a regular purl stitch. Purl the two stitches as one, creating one less stitch.

SLIP, SLIP, KNIT (SSK)

To create a left-slanting decrease, slip the first stitch as if to knit, slip the second stitch as if to knit, and then bring the left needle through both stitches from front to back and knit them together.

INCREASES

KNIT ONE IN FRONT AND BACK (KFB)

An easy way to increase is to knit one in the front and back of a stitch (kfb). To make this type of increase, simply insert your right-hand needle into the next stitch on the left-hand needle and knit the stitch, keeping the stitch on the left-hand needle instead of sliding it off. Then bring your right-hand needle around to the back, knit into the back loop of the same stitch, and slip both stitches off the needle. See page 15 in the Learning the Basics section for illustrated instructions on kfb.

MAKE ONE (M1)

With your right-hand needle, pick up the bar between two stitches from the front to the back, and place it on the left-hand needle, then knit it through the back loop. See page 15 in the Learning the Basics section for illustrated instructions on make one.

MATTRESS STITCH

Mattress stitch is a way of seaming two pieces of knitted fabric together. It creates an invisible seam by replicating the stitches on either side of the seam using a yarn needle and the same yarn used to create the knitted piece. Since most of the pieces in this book are worked in the round, there aren't many seams to sew up. See page 20 in the Learning the Basics section for illustrated instructions on working in mattress stitch.

PICKING UP STITCHES

To pick up a stitch, insert the tip of one needle through the side of a stitch from front to back. Leaving about a 3" to 4" (8cm to 10cm) tail, wrap yarn around the needle as you would for a regular knit stitch. Bring the yarn through the stitch, creating a loop on your needle. This loop is the first picked-up stitch. Continue to pick up the number of stitches required, making sure to space them evenly.

PLACING (AND SLIPPING) A MARKER (PM AND SM)

Sometimes a pattern calls for you to place a marker (pm) and slip a marker (sm). Markers are generally small plastic rings that slide onto a needle and rest in between stitches, marking a certain spot. If you don't have markers on hand, cut small pieces of scrap yarn in a contrasting color. Tie the scrap yarn around the needle in the indicated spot in a loose knot. Move the marker from one needle to the other when you come to it. Continue as usual.

PLACING STITCHES ON A HOLDER

For some of the patterns in this book, you'll be instructed to place a certain number of stitches onto a holder as you continue to work the remaining stitches. You may buy a stitch holder and slide the stitches onto it, or just use a piece of scrap yarn in a contrasting color. The stitches will be picked back up at the end, or seamed up.

STITCHES

GARTER STITCH

Garter stitch is created by knitting every single row when knitting back and forth on straight needles. If you're working in the round, you'll need to alternate between one knit row and one purl row to create garter stitch.

RIBBING

To create ribbing, simply alternate between knitting and purling. You can create a one-by-one rib, a two-by-two rib, a one-by-three rib...etc.! Ribbing is often used for sweater waistbands, cuffs and neckbands, and also for hat brims.

SEED STITCH

Seed stitch is a simple stitch that creates an interesting texture. Seed stitch is worked by knitting all purl stitches and purling all knit stitches. Here's how it works:

FOR AN ODD NUMBER OF STITCHES

ROW 1: * k1, p1; rep from * until last st, k1.

Rep Row 1.

FOR AN EVEN NUMBER OF STITCHES

ROW 1: * k1, p1*, rep from * until end of row.

ROW 2: * p1, k1; rep from * until end of row.

Rep Rows 1 and 2.

SINGLE CROCHET

On the right side of the fabric, with the edge facing away from you, insert the hook into the top edge of the stitch, wrap the yarn over the hook and pull it through the fabric. * Insert the hook into the next stitch, wrap the yarn over the hook, pull it through the fabric and through the loop on the hook. Rep from * to create a border as desired.

STOCKINETTE STITCH

To create stockinette stitch, knit on the right side and purl on the wrong side. If you're knitting in the round, knitting every row produces effortless stockinette with no purling.

YARN OVER (YO)

A yarn over is as easy as it sounds. When you come to a yarn over in the pattern, simply wrap the working yarn around the right-hand needle and continue knitting as usual. On the following row, you will knit or purl the wrapped yarn, creating an extra stitch and also an attractive eyelet hole in the knitted fabric. Because a yarn over creates a new stitch, a row with yarn overs is often combined with decreases.

WORKING IN THE ROUND

WITH CIRCULAR NEEDLES

Before you begin, make sure that your circular needles are a bit shorter than the diameter of your project. Simply cast on the requisite number of stitches just as you would on straight needles. Also make sure the stitches are not twisted. Hold the needle with the tail dangling from it in your left hand. Push the stitches to the end of the needle. Hold the needle with the working yarn in your right hand, push-

ing the first stitches to the end of that needle. Insert the tip of the right needle into the first stitch on the left needle from front to back. Wrap the working yarn around the right needle and knit your first stitch. Voilá, you're connected! After that, knit every row to produce Stockinette stitch.

WITH DOUBLE-POINTED NEEDLES

You may also knit in the round with DPNs. After casting on and dividing the stitches evenly over four needles, arrange the DPNs in a square shape, with the first cast-on stitch on the needle on the left, and with the final cast-on stitch on the needle adjacent to the first needle on the right of it. Insert the tip of the fifth needle into the first cast-on stitch, then wrap the working yarn from the adjacent right-side needle and knit as for a regular knit stitch.

WITH TWO SETS OF CIRCULAR NEEDLES

Since it's tough to find circular needles with a connector shorter than 12" (30cm), it's a neat trick to avoid the problem by knitting in the round with two sets of circular needles. This technique allows you to knit in the round regardless of the diameter. To knit in the round with this technique, cast on the required number of stitches, then slip half of the stitches as if to purl from one circular needle to a second circular needle. Move both sets of stitches to one end of each circular needle so the stitches line up. Before joining the stitches, slip the first stitch from the back needle onto the front needle, and slip the first stitch from the front needle onto the back needle so the two stitches trade places. Switching the position of the stitches helps stop the tube from gaping at the join. Grab the needle end attached to the front needle. Slip the tip of the needle into the first stitch on the front needle to prepare for a knit stitch. Grab the working yarn attached to the back needle and knit. After knitting all the stitches on the front needle, you'll rotate the work to continue working in the round to knit the second half of the stitches on the second needle. To knit these stitches, use the tail of the second needle. Continue knitting as before. Don't transfer stitches like you do when working with double-pointed needles. Always knit the stitches on the front needle with the other end of the front needle, and likewise with the stitches on the back needle. See page 16 in the Learning the Basics section for illustrated instructions on knitting in the round with two circular needles.

Resource Guide

The yarn and supplies used to make the projects in this book are manufactured by the following companies. In many cases, you can purchase the yarn directly from the manufacturers themselves, but sometimes you may need to reference their Web sites for the names and locations of vendors. Or do a quick online search for the name of the yarn to find an online vendor.

Adriafil
www.adriafil.com/index.html
Wild Things (page 132)

Blue Sky Alpaca Yarns
www.blueskyalpacas.com
Zip-Up Tassel Vests (page 60), Floppy Cat + Dog Stuffed Toys (page 64), Bulky Hand-Dyed Backpack + Matching Mom Tote (page 142), Animal Appliqué Totes (page 146)

Berroco Yarns
www.berroco.com
Baby Hats + Matching Mitts (page 36), Rollneck Giraffe Sweater (page 40), Fuzzy Bolero Sweater (page 86), Shaggy Vest (page 90), Royal Felted Slippers + Crowns (page 108), Fluffy Muffs + Matching Headband (page 124)

Cascade Yarns
www.cascadeyarns.com
Stretchy I-Cord Hats (page 28), Striped Vests (page 98), Castle Purse + Finger Puppets (page 102), Bath Time Fun Washcloths (page 116)

Classic Elite Yarns
www.classiceliteyarns.com
Fruity Bibs (page 32)

Crystal Palace Yarns
www.straw.com
Pup + Cat Pocket Scarf + Matching Hat Sets (page 112), Foxy Stoles (page 120), Funky Leg Warmers + Hair Scrunchie (page 128)

Debbie Bliss
www.debbieblissonline.com
Happily-Ever-After Dress (page 50), Fairy-Tale Dolls (page 54), Chunky Poncho (page 82)

Denise
www.knitdenise.com
interchangeable knitting needle set

Knit One, Crochet Too, Inc.
www.knitonecrochettoo.com
Shark Pullover (page 94)

The Knitting Experience Café
www.theknittingexperience.com
Brunswick, Maine, yarn store

Lantern Moon
www.lanternmoon.com
knitting needles and other knitting supplies (pictured on pages 6 and 10)

Lorna's Laces
www.lornaslaces.net
Tie-On Asymmetrical Sweater (page 70)

Malabrigo Yarn
www.malabrigoyarn.com
Swing Jacket (page 74), Handy Mittens (page 78)

Mission Falls
www.missionfalls.com
Cotton Baby Doll Top + Matching Purse (page 46)

Plymouth Yarns
www.plymouthyarn.com
Peek-a-Boo Bear Stroller Blanket (page 24)

Seaport Yarns
www.seaportyarn.com
Portland, Maine, yarn store

Sirdar
www.sirdar.co.uk
Hand Puppet Trio (page 136)

Index

CHECK OUT THESE OTHER FABULOUS TITLES FROM F+W PUBLICATIONS, INC.

PLUSH YOU!
BY KRISTEN RASK

The wildly popular Plush You! show is now available in book form, with pictures of each contribution, along with entertaining features such as plushie bios. This showcase of 100 plush toys, many with patterns and instructions, will inspire you to join in on the DIY toy phenomenon. The simple projects in this book provide instant gratification for beginners and new ideas and inspiration for experienced, full-time toymakers. Stuffed space creatures and lovable monsters, along with the occasional cut of beef and other squeezable subjects, make this an irresistibly hip book you'll just want to hug.

ISBN-13: 978-1-58180-996-1
ISBN-10: 1-58180-996-4
PAPERBACK WITH FLAPS, 144 PAGES, Z0951

MR. FUNKY'S SUPER CROCHET WONDERFUL
BY NARUMI OGAWA

Mr. Funky's Super Crochet Wonderful is filled with 25 supercute crochet patterns for adorable Japanese-style stuffed animals and accessories. You'll find candy-color elephants, panda bears, kitty cats, hamsters and even a snake, plus fashionable hats and purses for girls of all ages. Each pattern features written instructions as well as traditional Japanese crochet diagrams.

ISBN-13: 978-1-58180-966-4
ISBN-10: 1-58180-966-2
PAPERBACK WITH FLAPS, 112 PAGES, Z0697

YARNPLAY
BY LISA SHOBHANA MASON

YarnPlay shows you how to fearlessly mix yarns, colors and textures to create bold and graphic handknits. You'll learn how to draw from your yarn stash to create stylish, colorful knits, including sweaters, tanks, hats, scarves, blankets, washcloths and more for women, men and children. Best of all, you'll learn knitting independence—author Lisa Shobhana Mason believes in learning the rules so you can break them. She teaches you how to take a pattern and make it your own.

ISBN-13: 978-1-58180-841-4
ISBN-10: 1-58180-841-0
PAPERBACK WITH FLAPS, 128 PAGES, Z0010

These books and other fine F+W Publications, Inc. titles are available at your local craft retailer, bookstore or from online suppliers, including www.fwbookstore.com.